Double
Menopause

Double Menopause

What to Do When
Both You and Your Mate
Go Through Hormonal Changes
Together

Nancy Cetel, M.D.

JOHN WILEY & SONS, INC.

For general information about our other products and services, please contact our
Customer Care Department within the United States at (800) 762-2974, outside
the United States at (317) 572-3993 or fax (317) 572-4002.

Wiley also publishes its books in a variety of electronic formats. Some content that
appears in print may not be available in electronic books.

ISBN 0-471-40262-1

10   9   8   7   6   5   4   3   2   1

Contents

Acknowledgments   vii

Introduction   1

Part I   Menopause and Andropause under One Roof   7

1   Dueling Hormones   9

2   Female Menopause   21

3   Andropause: The Male Change   45

Part II   Dealing with Your Partner's Hormones   65

4   Midlife Sexuality: The Female Perspective   67

5   Midlife Sexuality: The Male Perspective   85

6   Understanding and Embracing This Important Time   99

7   A Woman's Guide to Surviving Her Man's Midlife Change   127

8   A Man's Guide to Surviving His Woman's Midlife Change   143

Part III   Getting to Hormonal Harmony   161

  9   Midlife Romance   163
10   Be Prepared If Turbulence Strikes   175
11   The Truth about Anti-Aging   193

Bibliography   219
References   225
Index   233

Acknowledgments

This book would not have been written without the encouragement and insistence of my patients. I have treated women with hormonal problems for over 20 years. Throughout that time it became abundantly evident that women are not the only ones who experience a hormonal and psychological change of life. Yet, there was very little information available that addressed the issue of a "male menopause." The more I searched for appropriate and useful reading material to recommend to my patients and their significant others, the more apparent it became that there was a void in the literature.

I began to write bits and pieces of informative and helpful advice for my patients and their mates. I had also been lecturing across the country. Inevitably, at the conclusion of my talks, members of the audience would beg for references to specific books that address both topics of male and female menopause together. I was always at a loss because I had yet to find one. That's when I was confronted with a gentle but firm plea to fill the void by writing a book about double menopause. So I thank my many patients and attendees at my lectures for their persistence that this book needed to be written.

Writing a book is a bit like going through a prolonged pregnancy. There are several stages that must be achieved before the actual delivery. Moving from concept to final product takes a significant amount of energy, time, and the involvement of many wonderful people. Without the help of my literary agent, Judith Riven, *Double Menopause* might still be a concept. She had the foresight that this was an important subject and the belief that it needed to be presented to the public. More importantly, she had the experience to help guide the project from proposal to acceptance. I also would like to thank Caron Golden for her help and encouragement in the early stages of this literary pregnancy.

I especially wish to thank the professional staff at John Wiley & Sons—Thomas Miller, my executive editor, who always seemed to have brilliant insight and creative suggestions; Kimberly Monroe, associate managing editor, and Jude Patterson, copy editor, for their eagle eyes and thoroughness in shaping the manuscript; and the design team for their artistic skills. They were all critical for the successful gestation and birth of this book.

I also wish to thank my colleagues and mentors at the School of Medicine, University of California, San Diego, Department of Reproductive Endocrinology. Drs. Samuel S. C. Yen and M. E. Ted Quigley, in particular, provided guidance and wisdom during my research into the marvels and mysteries of human reproductive endocrinology.

Last, but definitely not least, I want to thank the people in my personal life who helped me throughout all the stages of *Double Menopause*. To my wonderful husband, Joseph, who constantly provided encouragement and good humor, and who affectionately became my "poster boy" for male menopause. To my remarkable children, Danielle, Jeremy, and Lizzy, who provided Mom with love and support and even contributed with background research. To my good friends for their unwavering support—even when it looked like there was no end in sight. And to my personal energizers, Carol and

Scott Ross, Lee Postner, and the staff at Personally Fit who helped keep me fit, and sane, for the duration of the gestation.

A special word of thanks to my parents, Clara and Ben Cetel, who always encouraged me in all of my endeavors and instilled the love of learning forever. Without them, this book would not have been born.

Double Menopause

Introduction

It was becoming all too common. A well-established midlife couple with everything to be grateful for—a beautiful family, a cozy home, a comfortable lifestyle—and a divorce proceeding heatedly under way. Another midlife marital casualty. Not only was I observing this disturbing trend in my practice, but I saw friends' marriages disintegrating after 20 years of love and harmony. Was this midlife strife, midlife angst, or midlife crisis spinning out of control? Or was something more basic and even preventable occurring?

Many of my female patients were confiding that even though their hormone problems were under control, they felt that their husbands were having midlife problems, too. Worse yet, there was no one that their partners could talk with or consult with. Could I at least recommend some reading material that could help them and their husbands? That's when my quest began. The more I looked for information that I could offer my patients and their significant others about his and her midlife changes, the more I realized there was a void in the literature.

My patients convinced me that there was a true need for such a book, and the concept for *Double Menopause: What to Do When*

I

Both You and Your Mate Go Through Hormonal Changes Together was born. When I told my patients that I was writing about the male and female hormonal, psychological, and emotional challenges that affect all midlife couples (whether they know it or not), the response was overwhelmingly positive.

Having husbands accompany their wives for a midlife hormone consultation can be a very rewarding and revealing experience. When 54-year-old Roger came to the office with his wife of 22 years, he assumed he was being supportive of her menopausal transition. Indeed, Mimi was 50 years old and having hot flashes, sleep disturbances, and a complete loss of patience with everyone around her, especially Roger. As Roger put it, "I'm here to show Mimi that I care about her situation and I want to learn more about a woman's change of life."

I commended him on his empathy and desire to become a better informed, more understanding spouse. As the interview progressed and I was asking Mimi about changes in her sleep patterns, her memory, and her ability to concentrate, I could see Roger nodding his head up and down affirmatively at every question. I finally turned to him and asked, "So, Roger, do you tend to see Mimi having problems in all of these areas?"

"Well, I'm not so sure about Mimi, but I know that I've been having a lot of trouble sleeping and concentrating lately. And yes, I even feel warm and flushed at night, too. Could a man like myself get these problems, too?" It had never dawned on Roger or Mimi that he might be going through a form of male menopause at the same time that Mimi was going through her change. I reassured them both that it was perfectly normal, and far more common than people realize, and that men have their own version of midlife transition, often referred to as *andropause*. And while andropause is not the equivalent of menopause, there are many similarities that affect a man's physical and emotional well-being.

Roger almost fell from the stool he was perched on. He was

shocked that he hadn't heard about this before. Even his own physician hadn't discussed it with him. And though he typically didn't talk about this type of stuff with his buddies, he felt sure that many of them were having similar experiences. Since he was an activist type of guy, he decided right there and then to start a men's club to give men a forum to talk about their changes and get some information and help. He asked me to be their first presenter. At this point, I almost fell off my stool. Mimi's menopause consultation was turning into the launch of a men's health support group. I told him I would think about it but our first priority at the moment was to take care of Mimi and her needs and to bring him up to speed on her change of life. He apologized for jumping the gun, but I thanked him for his enthusiasm and agreed that much needed to be done to help men and couples going through this transition together.

In my over 20 years of caring for patients and conducting clinical research in reproductive endocrinology, I continue to observe and respect the undeniable link between hormones and midlife dynamics. It's becoming increasingly common to have a 40-something patient consult me for hormone therapy and sadly confide that, inexplicably, things are becoming shaky at home. Indeed, for these women and their partners, the hormonal and midlife connection is more than a link; it's a fact of life. And neither partner has any idea what's going on. In *Double Menopause* I address the emotional and psychological reactions as well as the physiological changes men and women experience with their unique midlife changes. This is definitely a book for both men and women. Midlife change is certainly not a women-only issue.

Couples struggling with each other during midlife is nothing new; but for generations it was understood— even joked about—as being caused by "the change"—definitely a woman's condition. It has been only recently, however, that we have come to understand that men, too, suffer from hormonal changes. Often called andropause and occurring between ages 40 and 65, the concept of a man's hormonal transition has recently been a headline grabber nationally and internationally.

With the onslaught of media attention for Viagra, the first impotency pill for men, male menopause was finally out of the closet and boomers were racing toward bookstores and pharmacies for answers and solutions. The intense enthusiasm for the promise of Viagra symbolizes the hunger and desire for instant cures to couples' very intimate problems. Even the most solid relationship can be rocked by impotency and other dilemmas. *Double Menopause* addresses these painful challenges and demystifies the physiological and psychological changes integral to midlife for men and women.

Double Menopause is divided into three sections with 11 topical chapters. Part I, "Menopause and Andropause under One Roof," begins by identifying the aging process baby boomer couples face. Chapter 1 goes behind the scenes to uncover another reality, why inevitable hormonal changes can undermine seemingly stable relationships and lead to alarmingly high divorce rates after 20-plus years of marriage. Chapters 2 and 3 provide important information for understanding the signs and symptoms of andropause and menopause for both men and women. Questionnaires help you and your partner understand if she is in menopause or if he is experiencing andropause. Strategies are provided to help you discuss these changes and potential treatment options with your physician.

Almost everybody experiencing midlife changes secretly worries whether they have lost their sex appeal and if their mate is looking around for someone younger or more attractive. Part II, "Dealing with Your Partner's Hormones," discusses the myths, fantasies, and realities of midlife sexuality in response to the physical and psychological changes of menopause and andropause. Chapters 4 and 5 examine the issues from the male and female perspective in turn. We all know about the waning of estrogen and testosterone, but there are other important factors that can affect libido and behavior. Chapter 6, "Understanding and Embracing This Important Time," explores why hormones represent the "ultimate" mind-body connection and why men are just as vulnerable to hormonal changes as women. Chapters 7 and 8 are survival guides to midlife change from the partner's point of view.

In Part III, "Getting to Hormonal Harmony," readers learn fun, practical, and effective techniques to ignite their midlife love hormones (Chapter 9, "Midlife Romance") and strategies to smooth the inevitable midlife conflicts that occur in relationships (Chapter 10, "Be Prepared If Turbulence Strikes"). Chapter 11, "The Truth about Anti-Aging," distinguishes the myths and the reality of what anti-aging medicine has to offer. Besides the sex hormones estrogen and testosterone, there are other important hormones that become reduced as we get older and can affect our physical and mental well-being. The pros and cons of supplementing such hormones as DHEA and growth hormone are discussed. By weaving the best of Western medical advice with the best of complementary options, the chapter offers a varied menu for optimal health at midlife and beyond.

Double Menopause addresses the needs and anxieties of stressed meno-boomer couples by handling your unique medical and psychological concerns with wisdom, compassion, reassurance, and cutting-edge information. A healthy, proactive mind-set lays the foundation for a positive and practical approach. This is a book to be read by men and women both, as much for your partner and your relationship as for yourself. You will learn how to appreciate each other's passages for their similarities, differences, and vulnerabilities as well as contribute to each other's well-being and that of your relationship. I have written *Double Menopause* to offer both reference and support for men and women wanting to understand and love their mate, cherish their relationship, and prevent "until hormones do us part." Amen.

PART I

MENOPAUSE AND ANDROPAUSE UNDER ONE ROOF

CHAPTER I

Dueling Hormones

The following self-guided questionnaire will help you and your partner identify potential double-menopause danger zones in your relationship and will provide the first stepping-stones in achieving successful remedies.

Identifying Double-Menopause Danger Zones

Please answer yes or no.

1. My partner and I are comfortable discussing our health concerns with each other.
2. I suspect my partner is having an affair.
3. I am upset that my partner is looking older.
4. I feel my partner is in good psychological health.
5. I often feel alone.
6. My partner seems edgy or frequently moody.
7. My partner makes me feel good about myself.
8. My partner is comfortable with his/her sex life.

9. I feel close and connected with my partner.

10. I place a high value on keeping in good physical condition.

11. My partner and I are both following "healthy" diets.

12. Both of us have had a physical exam within the last year.

13. I feel in good physical health.

14. I feel in good psychological health.

15. My partner and I are pleased with our weight.

16. My partner is comfortable with his/her physical condition.

17. I see signs of aging in myself and feel desperate for plastic surgery.

18. My partner places a high value on keeping in good physical condition.

19. I see signs of aging in my partner and I am comfortable with this.

20. My partner resents/fears getting older.

21. I sleep soundly and wake up refreshed.

22. I am satisfied with my energy levels.

23. I feel good about myself.

24. I often feel depressed.

25. My partner is interested in learning about how the change of life can affect my health and well-being.

26. I am comfortable with my sex life.

27. Our relationship brings me comfort.

28. I am generally even-tempered.

29. My partner seems depressed.

30. I resent/fear getting older.

31. I am happy with my work or retirement.

32. I often feel irritable.

33. I feel financially secure.

34. I feel my partner is in good physical health.

35. My partner frequently tells me I am looking older or tired.
36. We both look forward to sexual intimacy.
37. I feel emotionally close with my partner.
38. My partner and I are able to talk about sensitive issues.
39. I still find my partner physically attractive.
40. I am fearful my partner desires a younger mate.
41. My partner and I enjoy each other's company.
42. I am interested in understanding how the change of life can affect my partner's health and well-being.
43. I see signs of aging in my partner and that makes me feel old.

Multiply by a factor of 1 any yes answers for questions 2–3, 5, 6, 17, 20, 24, 29–30, 32, 35–36, 40, 43. Multiply by a factor of 2 any no answers for questions 1, 4, 7–16, 18–19, 21–23, 25–28, 31, 33–34, 37–39, and 41–42. Add your total yes points and no points separately.

SCORES 0–10: Picture perfect—too good to be true!
         11–20: Smooth sailing ahead—keep up the good work!
         21–45: Imminent danger, but awareness helps—strategies will be necessary.
         46–70: Fasten your seatbelt, turbulent conditions—employ emergency strategies as soon as possible!

A Tale of Two Menopauses

"If only he had started on hormones when I began Premarin, none of this would have happened," Jan said, referring to the nasty breakup of a seemingly picture-perfect 26-year-long marriage. He was a successful corporate executive, she a devoted stay-at-home wife and mother with two grown kids and a beautiful home in the suburbs. Although it looked like they had it all, something was missing.

When 49-year-old Jan began to feel edgy, irritable, and depressed, she consulted with her physician. The diagnosis was perimenopause transition and she began a low-dose regimen of hormone replacement. Her normally cheerful disposition returned and she felt back to normal. By the time she realized that Bob, her 53-year-old lifelong mate, was experiencing similar symptoms, it was too late.

Instead of communicating, Bob withdrew. He stayed at work later and later. Their sex life, which had been dwindling for some time, became nonexistent. At first Jan was relieved because her sexual desire was lacking, but after her doctor diagnosed the change of life and supplemented her hormones, her libido came alive. But what about Bob? He emphatically denied anything was wrong. As a matter of fact, the more Jan realized that he was not himself, the more distant the relationship became. When Jan discovered Bob's ongoing relationship with a woman half his age, it dawned on her that she knew nothing about the changes that occur in a man's mind, body, and spirit at midlife. Bob was living in denial and Jan was helplessly standing by. The divorce papers brought them both into crisp reality.

While at a recent escape to a luxury health spa to heal herself, Jan realized that her only regret is not recognizing the subtle, and sometimes not so subtle, signs of male menopause and how it affected both Bob and their relationship. Perhaps medical and/or psychological intervention could have helped. With a twinge of guilt, Jan reminisced, "I was so wrapped up in my own hormonal changes I didn't even notice Bob's."

Sometimes it is impossible to see the full extent of a problem if one is wearing blinders. Jan fully admits that she was so focused on her own menopausal hormonal dilemmas that she did not pick up on the menopausal changes that Bob was experiencing. In fact, she regrets not having the basic knowledge that her husband could even be experiencing something similar to her own change of life, both hormonally and psychologically. She simply wasn't aware that such a thing as a male menopause even existed. "If only I had known," she laments, "we both would have been better prepared to make the journey together. Instead, I went my way and he went his. Neither of us had a clue about what the other was experiencing."

Unfortunately, lack of knowledge of age-related hormonal changes as well as lack of acknowledgment are both common culprits in the unraveling of long-term marital bonds. Sometimes the elements of denial and/or fear by one or both partners can push a relationship over the edge. Neither husband nor wife is happy with the way their lives are going, yet they are unable to communicate their feelings to one another. Avoidance takes precedence over communication and lays the foundation for withdrawal and isolation. Each partner develops his or her own perceptions of the other, with neither daring to reveal any fears or frustrations. These silent perceptions can lead to misconceptions that put seasoned relationships in the double-menopause danger zone. Acknowledging these perceptions is the first step toward averting marital disaster.

His perceptions:
- She seems edgy, tired, and irritable.
- She doesn't seem to be as interested in me as she used to be.
- Sex isn't as spontaneous. What happened to the excitement?
- Am I still as capable as I used to be?
- Our relationship is changing in uncomfortable ways.
- It's her menopause and I better not mess with her.

Her perceptions:
- He seems edgy, tired, and irritable.
- He doesn't seem to be as interested in me as he used to be.
- Sex isn't as enjoyable. I've lost my interest and he is embarrassed that he is having trouble in that department.
- Is he depressed or having a midlife crisis?
- Our relationship is changing in uncomfortable ways.
- He doesn't find me attractive anymore.

Acknowledging and becoming knowledgeable about each other's midlife hormonal changes is a necessary first step to avert a hormone-induced breakup. When a man becomes educated about the hormonal changes a woman experiences during menopause, he is transformed from a helpless mate to a helpmate. His sense of power-lessness transforms itself into empowerment and he no longer feels bewildered and intimidated by the process. Likewise, when a woman becomes educated and aware that her man is not immune from a midlife hormonal transition, she, too, becomes empowered to be a better helpmate and can tune in to the subtle changes.

What Do Hormones Have to Do with It?

As a gynecologist and reproductive endocrinologist, I believe hor-mones make the world go round. And when they are out of whack, so, too, is our personal world. I came to this understanding at a rela-tively young age—many years prior to my formal studies in medical school, internship, residency training, and fellowship in the field of reproductive endocrinology and infertility.

At the age of 16, I learned firsthand how an instant of terror can produce a year of hormonal dysfunction. While I was not physically harmed, I had become psychologically traumatized by witnessing a mugging walking home from high school on a late autumn after-noon. And although the potential for true bodily harm was very real, I managed to escape from a dangerous situation and call for help. After the episode, I was quite relieved to learn that the victim was not seriously hurt and I went back to my normal day-to-day living—or so I thought. Little did I anticipate the aftermath of my moment of terror.

For one full year after "the event," as I've come to refer to the mugging incident, my menstrual periods disappeared. I was a puzzle to my general doctor and I baffled the specialist to whom I was re-ferred. I was a mystery to the medical profession—but deep within the confines of my adolescent psyche, within the neurochemical and neuroendocrinological chambers of my brain—lay the answer. I felt it was up to me to solve this puzzle and help myself. And I did.

Once I consciously acknowledged what had happened and linked the event to the aftermath of no periods, my normal menstrual cycle resumed. I had experienced firsthand the power of the mind-body connection and the interaction between the psyche and hormonal function. My body had responded physically to the neurochemical signals induced by sheer terror and temporarily shut down my reproductive system. It was as if the mind was letting the body know that events in the environment were too tense, abnormal, and too dangerous for a pregnancy. So the endocrine system picked up the message and literally shut down the normal hormonal messengers necessary for ovulation and menstruation.

Only when there was a conscious acknowledgment and subsequent release of subconscious fear did my hormonal system restore itself to normal. This intimate link, just one example of a mind-body connection, also illustrates the hormonal or endocrine system's feedback loop. Without this loop none of us could function. And when this loop is thrown off track, even subtly, it can affect our daily lives. If we ignore it, the problem persists—as happened to me with a cesssation of my periods. If we are tuned in to the changes and acknowledge these events in our lives, we can choose to live and communicate more effectively.

What Both Sexes Must Know about Each Other's Hormonal Changes

Male menopause has always existed but only recently has it been acknowledged and given its own identity as andropause. It is not the equivalent to female menopause, but many men lose potency, energy, and drive between 40 and 80 years of age. Although there is a definite and significant decline in the circulating blood levels of the male sex hormone testosterone, there is not a complete halt to production as there is for estrogen in women. In fact, many men still retain their fertility into old age in contrast to women, who lose reproductive function by age 50. This biological discrepancy between the sexes gives a man a psychological and physiological edge by maintaining a link to the mythical fountain of youth through potentially limitless reproductive capacity. Pablo Picasso, Marlon Brando, Larry King, and Saul Bellow are prominent examples of men who fathered children at an advanced age—all with much younger female partners.

Similar to women in menopause, however, all andropausal men experience varying losses of decreased lean body mass, diminished muscle strength, reduced bone density, and loss in potency. There are psychological ramifications to these changes as well, which may manifest in fatigue, loss of libido, reduced sense of well-being, and depression. Often there are conflicting emotions. Previously repressed frustrations and anger may surface—to the dismay of both the man and his partner. With the lowering of critical hormone levels comes the lowering of the threshold of tolerance. This can become very frightening and threatening on both the home front and in the workplace, especially if it is not understood or anticipated. Recognizing these signals and responding with compassion and professional attention can not only preserve the relationship but also protect a man's health. A woman should be aware of these potential changes for the sake of her partner and their relationship.

Likewise, a man needs to recognize and understand a woman's change of life so that he can provide compassionate guidance and not be frightened away. A little knowledge can go a long way in alleviating fears—both his and hers. By understanding that a woman's change of life is a natural event related to declining estrogen levels, both partners can become involved in planning for this time of life. This typically occurs between the ages of 45 and 53 with predictable symptoms—hot flashes, sleep disturbances, vaginal dryness, moodiness, change in menses—and there are many treatment options available. I encourage men to join their partners when they visit a health care provider for menopause consultation, not only to provide emotional support for their partner, but to take the opportunity to learn more about the physical and emotional changes she is undergoing.

I am always pleased to see a man come into the office with his significant other for the menopause or hormone consultation. In this protected environment, intimate matters can be freely discussed and questions answered that might not have surfaced before. A man may come to understand why his wife's libido has changed and what options are available to help them both. Perhaps her hot flashes are walking him up at night and she wasn't even aware. There needs to be an openness and a freedom to the discussion. On several occasions men have accompanied their wives to the office and told me about their hot flashes, something that they had never mentioned to anyone before, not even their own doctor.

The coupled office visit is an ideal opportunity that is too often overlooked. If you haven't tried it yet, I strongly recommend scheduling one and bringing a list of his and her questions. Preventing misconceptions and enhancing communication brings us closer to the overall goal of hormonal harmony—and it's never too late.

It Was His Hormones All Along

I had just given my seminar "Menopause: His, Hers, and Theirs" to a standing-room-only audience at a well-known health resort when a petite, fragile-appearing woman well into her 80s approached me.

"Dear," she said with a charming Southern accent, "you just made my day!"

"How so?" I asked, rather taken aback.

"Well, for the past thirty-some years," she said, "it always bothered me that no one believed me when I complained that my husband was going through some kind of menopause way back then. The doctors just laughed at me. I always believed poor John was going through some hormonal hell—bless his soul—and nobody would help him. He was so moody when he turned fifty, his sex drive just about dried up and he even had hot flashes! Of course he wouldn't admit to any of it and those doctors thought I was the crazy one. I'm happy to know from what you just told us here tonight that's exactly what his condition was—and it was no laughing matter! Too bad this knowledge came thirty years too late for him. The good news is I can still use this bit of information 'cause you see I'm working on my next fella! Thanks, dear, for letting me know I wasn't crazy after all." With that, this sweet octogenarian Southern belle gave me a hug and waltzed from the room.

Necessary Information for Contemporary Couples

Ron, a rugged-looking man in his 50s, sat in the front row and hung on to every word of my lecture about male menopause. When I finished speaking, much to his and the audience's surprise, he blurted, with a perplexed groan, "I wish someone had told me about this before the divorce!" Then, after the room cleared, he cautiously approached me. "You know, Doc, before I heard what you had to say, I didn't believe much in this hormone stuff." He took a deep breath and continued, "But now I see it differently. I just went through a divorce—after twenty-one years of marriage, no less. I'm an attorney. I'm seriously thinking of changing careers and I have every darn symptom on your list of male menopausal signs and symptoms! What do you think I should do?" For Ron, an immediate referral to a specialist was in order and he was relieved when I could refer him to someone in his hometown.

I have often been disturbed by the alarmingly high statistics for midlife divorce among couples married 20 years or more—over 50 percent. Having survived over two decades of life together as one half of a couple, as well as a family, conquering tragedies and celebrating triumphs together, I find it defies all logic that this would be a rational time to separate. Surely, society alone is not to blame. And while there are, of course, individual variations on the theme, there is more often than not a common thread—a hormonal link.

All midlife couples face turbulence. It is a matter of degree and preparedness that makes the difference between those who separate and those who compensate. Indeed, some midlife couples renew their vows and strengthen their identity as a pair. And what force could be so powerful as to either drive couples apart or solidly re-unite them? In the chapters that follow, you will discover your natu-ral role and learn strategies for achieving hormonal harmony until *death* do you part.

CHAPTER 2

Female Menopause

Most women accept the fact that menopause is a natural transition of life. Indeed, it is almost impossible to live in the twenty-first century and not have heard of the words *perimenopause* or *menopause*—unless one has led a very sheltered or isolated life. No longer shrouded in secrecy or restrained by embarrassment, menopause has become the power chant of the not so silent female meno-boomer population. The male constituents of this generation have, for the most part, remained behind in their caves. However, this, too, is changing, albeit slowly, as more light is shed on the subject.

What a difference a century has made! In the early 1900s, menopause was not a major topic of interest. With an average life expectancy of approximately 50 years, most women did not live beyond their reproductive years and didn't have to concern themselves with longevity issues. Now women are living up to 30 years and beyond their fertile time zone and have to worry about health issues such as heart disease, stroke, osteoporosis, hot flashes, mood disturbances, and assorted quality-of-life issues. No longer are their bodies and minds fueled by the ovarian release of estradiol.

In the last quarter of the twentieth century, menopause was catapulted from obscurity to celebrity status. Indeed, such female icons as Lauren Hutton, Cher, Goldie Hawn, and Cheryl Tiegs are but a few of the thoroughly modern meno-boomers who have shared their secrets and advice for negotiating this time of life. Lauren Hutton has become a spokeswoman for Wyeth Pharmaceuticals, extolling the benefits of hormone replacement therapy (HRT) with Premarin. Cheryl Tiegs has been the cover girl for *More,* a magazine dedicated to the female over-50 set. Indeed, today's menopausal woman has far many more role models than did their mothers, just one generation ago.

Mother's Little Helper

What a difference a generation makes! During the early 1950s if a woman was brave enough to consult with her doctor about the change, chances are she would have been treated with a healthy dose of the popular tranquilizer of that era, Librium, also affectionately known as "mother's little helper." A popular advertisement in the medical journals of that era depicts a male physician in a starched white coat seated behind an enormous wood desk with a timid and fretful middle-aged woman in front of him. The caption reads: "The Treatment of Choice for That Time of Life—Librium."

No wonder women didn't like talking about "that time of life" back then—there was limited information and the treatment was geared to calming them down. If a woman wasn't already feeling zombielike because of sleep deprivation caused by nighttime hot flashes disrupting her REM sleep (rapid eye movement, associated with dreams and psychological renewal during sleep), then the prescription tranquilizers were sure to zap her remaining energy.

Ready for Prime Time

Even Edith and Archie Bunker had to deal with menopausal issues in the memorable *All in the Family* TV series of the 1970s. During one episode Edith is experiencing hot flashes and is trying to explain to Archie why she is so moody and emotional. Archie, who has no clue or sensitivity, finally yells out, "For heaven's sake, Edith, why are you more of a dingbat than usual?"

Edith responds, "It's the change, Archie. Don't you understand, all women go through the change of life?"

Then, with his typical grace, Archie roars back, "Well then, Edith, go ahead and change. I'll give you five minutes, then let's get on with it!" Although Archie was far from any midlife male marital role model, this was cutting-edge material for 1970s prime-time television.

I remember feeling sorry for my mother. Because I was a much wanted, but late in life, baby, I was only nine years old when she went through the change in her late forties. I could not understand what the true situation was—women did not speak openly about menopause then—but I knew it was not fun.

My poor father was confused and somewhat frustrated, but did his best to protect my mother. When the hot flashes got particularly bad, her heart palpated and she would have to lie down. It was an ongoing event that we all lived through. The doctors at the time really didn't have much to offer and we all learned to cope. Although I truly didn't understand what was happening to my mother, I was told that all women at her age go through things like that and that eventually my mother would "come out of it." As an inquisitive nine-year-old girl I was unwittingly being primed for my professional future. Little did I know that 18 years later I would be on the doorstep of new frontiers in menopausal research.

The Science of Menopause Research

It was July 1, 1980, and as a brand-new fellow in the growing field of reproductive endocrinology, I was awed and thrilled to participate in such an exciting arena of medicine and science. Reproductive endocrinology is a specialty branch of obstetrics and gynecology dealing with hormonal problems as varied as infertility, precocious puberty, excessive hair growth, polycystic ovary syndrome, endometriosis, and menopause. During the early 1980s when I began my fellowship training at the University of California at San Diego, the world of reproductive endocrinology was being revolutionized by the advent of in vitro fertilization. IVF, as it was referred to, was nothing short of a miracle—especially for couples with long-standing infertility. Modern science, high technology, and medicine were all coming together to help produce test-tube babies for couples who had previously given up all hope of ever giving birth to their own child.

It was in this environment that I volunteered for and was selected to study the neuroendocrinology of the hot flash, while many of my male colleagues drooled over the more intriguing, cutting-edge projects involving IVF. My mother's and other menopausal women's miseries had not been for naught and I relished the thought of conquering hot flashes for all womankind. Yes, a heavy blend of optimism and enthusiasm was necessary to be a thorough and determined research fellow.

My first assignment was to help decipher the basic physiology of the hot flash. We had come a long way from the days of "It's all in your head," "Take some tranquilizers and you'll feel better," "All women have to go through this—you'll get through it eventually." This was medical science in the making. I felt that we were so much more enlightened in the 1980s than was the medical community of the 1950s because I knew that a hot flash was a real physiological event and not just an emotional aberration of semideranged middle-aged women. However, I admit that I was a bit naïve back then not to realize that enlightenment is an ongoing process, as we accumulate more knowledge and continuously refine our previously held beliefs and principles.

My volunteer patients were wonderful and truly dedicated to helping science unlock the mysteries of the hot flash. Each woman was admitted overnight to the Clinical Research Unit of the hospital after signing an informed consent form; that is, I would explain what the protocol would involve, how long they would be in the hospital, and what risks were involved such as potential discomfort or infection from placement of an intravenous line or drawing of blood samples over time. They were also told they could withdraw from the study at any time. All of the women had to be in menopause (verified by blood hormone levels) and not currently taking any form of hormone replacement.

The goal of the study was to understand and document in depth the physiological changes that would accompany the hot flash: What actually happened to the body's core temperature during a hot flash? What hormone changes occurred? What else was happening—did heart rate or blood pressure change? What about sleep disturbances? The women felt they were there for a cause and wanted answers. And so did I.

Each volunteer was monitored with a continuous temperature probe to record all temperature changes throughout the study. A small IV catheter was inserted into a vein to allow for minute samples of blood to be withdrawn painlessly at regular intervals. This would allow detection of moment-to-moment changes in hormone levels before, during, and after a hot flash. The temperature probe was also hooked up to a recording device that would monitor fluctuations in body temperature similar to seismographic recordings before, during, and after an earthquake. Indeed, some of the hot flashes were severe enough to jolt a woman out of a sound sleep almost as if she were experiencing a bodily earthquake.

Hot Flashes That Chill

One patient, Ann, a 49-year-old divorced real estate broker, had heard about the ongoing studies from a friend who had been an earlier volunteer. She was suffering miserably from hot flashes for the past three months and her personal physician wanted her to start hormone therapy. "Not until after I dedicate myself to science will I start any hormone therapy," she told me during the initial interview and screening process. She understood that she would disqualify herself by being on hormones and her determination to be part of the study prevailed. Ann was admitted for a 24-hour study one week later.

Ann's hot flashes were some of the most potent I have ever witnessed. Not only would her neck, face, and head turn crimson, but her entire body would be drenched in perspiration. She looked like a perpetually wilted flower. It was an understatement to say that these size 10 seismic hot flashes were interfering with her daily living—not to mention the nights. Almost like clockwork, at 90-minute intervals, the temperature recorder would jump and then drop below baseline as Ann experienced a surge of heat followed by an outpouring of perspiration. It was an if her own body were trying to put out a fire with a built-in sprinkler system. It was not surprising that she was experiencing chills after the hot flashes. Sometimes she would wake up completely and other times she would toss about and not appear to be fully alert.

Nevertheless, the temperature recordings and the blood hormone changes measured throughout the night documented the synchrony and regularity of these hot flash explosions. No wonder she felt sleep deprived, irritable, and not her usual perky self. Night after night of sleep loss can cause mood changes, depression, memory loss, cognitive impairment, greater vulnerability to accidents, and even illness.

No wonder Ann was not feeling herself. When she saw her study results—great spikes in the temperature graph and simultaneous spikes in brain hormone levels as her body tried desperately to order the ovaries to squeeze out a bit more estrogen—she half joked that she felt as erratic as the lab tests looked. Fortunately, we were able to restore Ann's estrogen levels with a small amount of natural estrogen and her hot flashes and sleepless nights became a distant memory.

Tired of Waiting

Emma was a 60-year-old grandmother of eight who referred herself to the study because she wanted to know if we could predict when her hot flashes would finally quit. "I keep waiting for those darn things to leave me alone. Everyone says they eventually go away, but mine just won't quit. I'm getting so tired of them, some days I feel I could scream!" I could empathize with her, but I couldn't promise I would be able to predict her hot flash future. "Sign me up anyway," she bellowed. "After all these years maybe some good can come out of studying these nasty things."

It was not surprising that Emma's estrogen levels were quite low—so low that they were below the detection level of the blood assay. What was a surprise was that Emma managed to sleep through some significant changes in body temperature throughout the night. Although she was having hot flashes night and day, she was only conscious of the annoying daytime flashes that made her sweat "like a pig in bold sunlight," as she fondly described herself. Somehow her body had mercifully adapted to sleeping through the nighttime flashes. Perhaps that's how she was able to survive 10 years' worth of hot flashes while Ann felt she could not have tolerated another week.

When Menopause Is Sudden and Intense

Darlene was a 55-year-old breast cancer survivor whose uterus and ovaries had been removed six years ago. Within two days after the hysterectomy, she said, her hot flashes were "lightning intense." It is not unusual for women to experience extreme hot flashes after a surgical menopause. When the ovaries are abruptly removed at the time of surgery, the body and brain are left with an immediate hormone deficit. All the estrogen receptors in the brain are thrown into an instant "estrogen withdrawal" syndrome. There is no time to gradually adjust to declining estrogen levels as is the case during a natural perimenopause to menopausal transition.

Before she volunteered, Darlene's hot flashes had simmered down for a few years. Although she had never taken hormone therapy and was experiencing only occasional, mild hot flashes, she had heard about the study and wanted to participate. She was also curious how she compared with other women who had gone through a natural menopause. Because her ovaries had been surgically removed, there was no detectable estradiol. However, her pituitary hormone levels, LH (luteinizing hormone) and FSH (follicle-stimulating hormone) were just as high as those of the women whose ovaries were intact.

Since there is a feedback system between the hypothalamus (higher brain), pituitary gland (lower brain), and ovary to regulate the amount of estrogen in the bloodstream, when estrogen levels decline the brain calls down for more. As the levels of estrogen become lower, the LH and FSH levels rise. The pituitary gland and the hypothalamus do not know about a hysterectomy, they only know that the estrogen levels have suddenly disappeared from the bloodstream. The hot flash is felt to be a neuroendocrine, or brain/hormone, event triggered by neurotransmitters.

These neurotransmitters are released in the hypothalamus in close proximity to the body's temperature-regulating center, called the preoptic-anterior hypothalamic region, which in turn causes the thermostat to temporarily go haywire. The result is a distinct hot flash sensation as the body perceives sudden heat. Since overheating can cause damage to organs and brain (heat stroke), the body will automatically and almost immediately start the cool-down process to restore normal core temperature. The net effect is hot flashes, perspiration, moist clothes, and soggy hair. The body is indeed a remarkable machine.

Not All Menopauses Are Created Equal

Lila came to us because she was 53 years old, had stopped having periods two years ago, and was not having hot flashes. She was interested in knowing if she was really in menopause and if this was normal. As scientists we also were curious as to why some menopausal women have severe flashes while others don't seem to be bothered at all. In Lila's case, her estrogen levels were definitely very low and in the menopausal range. Because of the feedback system, her LH and FSH levels were high, as expected—and yet she didn't have hot flashes.

While monitoring her core body temperature, we noted some mild fluctuations throughout the day which coincided with the spikes of hormone changes that often accompany hot flashes in other women. It is possible that Lila's "mini" flashes were more like mild flushes that were barely detectable. We believe that this is not at all related to her hormone levels because they were in a similar range to those of women who have typical hot flashes. Nor do we believe that Lila was any more stoic than any other woman in the study. We can only theorize that there are slight variations in the anatomical geography of the brain such that the temperature-regulating center may be a bit further removed from the spillage of the neurotransmitters that trigger hot flashes. By the way, a hot flash is scientifically referred to as a *vasomotor* event because the blood vessels (vaso) dilate and constrict (motor). Whatever the name, once a woman experiences a hot flash, she won't forget the feeling.

I will always be grateful to all the women who generously contributed their time to the study of menopause and hot flashes. We learned a lot together and certainly have come a long way from the more clueless years of the early 1950s. However, the journey is not over. The research and studies continue. Women's health and menopause in particular are on the frontlines of continuous investigation. If only we had all the answers. But we don't. There are almost daily reports, often appearing contradictory, about the benefits or risks of hormone replacement therapy.

As a physician, a clinician, a researcher, and a woman going through her own hormonal challenges, I painfully acknowledge and appreciate the difficulties in sorting out the pros and cons of hormone replacement therapy. Once, after lecturing to a group of nurse practitioners, all medically educated women in their 40s and

50s, a woman came up to me and suggested I teach a course about hormones called "Truth or Consequences." I joked that I thought the title sounded a bit too threatening, although it made a valid point. Women deserve to know the truth about the pros and cons of hormone replacement therapy because their decisions will have consequences for their health.

Menopause and the Media

When a front-page newspaper headline shouts "New Study Shows Estrogen Linked to Breast Cancer" and the fine print reveals a small study of six women in a foreign country taking a form of estrogen not prescribed in the United States so that the results do not reach statistical significance, the effect is to alarm and not truly inform. Burying in the back section of that same newspaper on the same day a highly significant report that colon cancer is reduced by over 50 percent in menopausal women who had taken estrogen for at least five years sends a definite message that positive results are less newsworthy of front-page status than scary results. It also does a gross injustice to all women struggling to learn the truth.

Recently a major medical journal reported that women with menopausal symptoms who received hormone replacement therapy experienced improved verbal memory, vigilance, reasoning, and motor speed. With the advent of fMRI (functional magnetic resonance imaging) scans, which allow direct visualization of the brain during an activity such as recalling words or numbers, we can better assess the impact of estrogen on brain function.

An ongoing study referred to as SWAN (Study of Women's Health Across the Nation) seeks to provide more widespread understanding of the biological and psychosocial characteristics of the transition from pre- to postmenopause. By measuring such parameters as daily hormonal fluctuations, as well as daily changes in mood and behavior, we will have a better understanding of the basics of the perimenopausal transition.

Menopause and Soy

Cultural differences may also play a role. It has been thought that women living in Japan do not suffer from hot flashes as much as Western women. One popular theory attributes the cause to dietary differences, especially the consumption of miso or soy-based products by native Japanese women. Thus far most studies have not shown that eating soy-based products, which contain isoflavones, a natural estrogenlike substance, has a significant impact upon hot flashes.

Another explanation suggested itself to me while I was on a recent trip to Japan. After remarking about the apparent discrepancy between American women suffering from hot flashes in the United States and the lack of menopausal problems in Japan and Asia as a whole, a Japanese woman came up to whisper in my ear, "Here in Japan, Japanese women have many hot flashes, but we learn to persevere." That bit of insider information made me break out in my own hot flash. Have we been fooling ourselves into thinking soy reduces hot flashes when all along it's really been stoicism, denial, or a form of cultural inhibition?

Meant to Pause or Mental Pause?

I was lecturing one balmy evening to a group of 40- and 50-something ladies at a beautiful health spa in San Diego. The mood was one of relaxation, peace, and serenity. After all, these ladies had been spa'd out for the entire week with massages, facials, herbal wraps, and meditation. The essence of tranquility was in the air and the karma was contagious. I was waxing poetic about menopause and how this was a time in a woman's life when we're all meant to pause and be tuned in to our body's changes, when suddenly a sleepy woman in the back row bolted up and shrieked, "Did you say mental pause? I knew it was true that I was losing my mind!"

Before I could utter another syllable to correct the misquote, there was pandemonium in the audience. It was as if a raw nerve had been pinched and twisted. This was a woman's worst fear: losing her mind. Nothing that I had discussed up until this point had created such a stir. And while I denied saying "mental pause," I couldn't deny that there is tremendous interest and research in deciphering the impact of menopausal hormone changes on our minds, moods, and memories. Studies are also ongoing which are seeking to confirm how estrogen may or may not protect the brain from Alzheimer's, stroke, cognitive dysfunction, and lapses in memory.

Some compelling evidence is already available. In a prospective study of surgically induced menopausal women, researcher Barbara Sherwin showed that those women given estrogen postoperatively maintained their scores on varying tests of abstract reasoning and memory in contrast to placebo-treated women whose test scores decreased. Other studies have confirmed that estrogen plays a significant role in maintaining cognitive function as well as verbal memory in women.

There is also preliminary evidence that estrogen therapy initiated after the onset of menopause can have a neuroprotective effect against Alzheimer's disease even some 25 to 35 years later. It is believed that hot flashes can cause damage to the hippocampus, an area of the brain that is critical for learning and memory, in a woman's brain by decreasing blood flow to this region. As a result, this part of the brain has a reduced ability to compensate for the long-term neurodegenerative processes of aging and Alzheimer's disease. This explains scientific observations that estrogen use at the time of menopause appears to have a greater protective effect against neurodegenerative conditions than initiation at later stages in menopause.

Since multiple neural networks and functions are estrogen dependent, it is not surprising that lowering of estrogen levels within the central nervous system can lead to shifts in behavior and mood. The all too common complaints of irritability, anxiety, depression, trouble focusing on tasks, memory impairment, and sleep disruption may be the result of estrogen decline within neural networks. In some cases, insomnia and sleep disturbances may be the only presenting symptoms of perimenopausal transition.

In general, research has shown that in aging animals, estrogen plays an important role in maintaining the function of the hippocampus. Overall, estrogen is considered a neuroprotective agent for maintaining and nourishing dendrite (branchlike connections between nerve cells) growth. Further studies will hopefully reconfirm these encouraging results.

Preventing Osteoporosis

Osteoporosis is a preventable skeletal disease characterized by low bone mass and deteriorating bone tissue, and in which the bones are subject to increased fracture risk. Because bone loss is accelerated in women in the first few years after menopause, perimenopausal women should be assessed not only to determine potential risk but also to initiate preventive therapy. The greater our peak bone mass prior to menopause, the lower our subsequent risk. However, in comparison to men, women are at substantially higher risk for developing postmenopausal osteoporosis and subsequent hip fractures. Genetics, exercise, weight resistance, calcium consumption, dietary factors, and medical history all play a role in our ultimate bone density.

Risk factors for osteoporosis include sedentary lifestyle; petite, thin, or small frame; low calcium intake; smoking; history of excessive thyroid medication or hyperthyroidism; long-term steroid usage; excessive coffee, alcohol, or carbonated beverage consumption; and being of female gender—especially of Caucasian or Asian descent. Certain lifestyle factors can be modified, such as how much dietary calcium we consume and how much exercise we engage in. Outside of hormone replacement and pharmaceutical intervention, weight-bearing exercise, including walking and resistance training, provides the best general protection from bone loss.

Bone mineral density should be evaluated at the hip and spine to

determine potential risk for fractures. Dual-energy x-ray absorptiometry (DEXA) is a safe and accurate method for measurement
and is readily available at most major medical centers. The term
osteopenia is used to describe a decreased quantity of bone. The
greater the degree of osteopenia, the higher the risk of osteoporosis
and subsequent hip fractures.

For a 50-year-old woman, the risk of a hip fracture during her
lifetime is estimated to be 16 percent and the risk of a vertebral fracture is 32 percent. Unfortunately, if a woman sustains an osteoporotic
hip fracture, her risk for morbidity and even death goes up considerably. Eva Gabor was a vivacious 76-year-old who sustained a hip
fracture, and subsequently died in the hospital of additional compli-
cations. Because of her celebrity status, her condition was publicized. However, for many postmenopausal women this is too often a
silent epidemic. Osteoporosis can result in a hip fracture, subsequent
hospitalization, and a downhill spiral toward death. The statistics are
grim.

Besides dietary and lifestyle changes, several pharmaceutical
agents have been useful in the prevention and treatment of osteoporosis. Estrogen replacement therapy in combination with calcium
supplementation (1,000 mg daily if on HRT and 1,500 mg daily if not
on HRT) is the most common treatment. In addition, calcitonin,
sodium fluoride, vitamin D (400 IU daily), bisphosphonates such as
Fosamax that build bone mass, and parathyroid hormone have also
been proven effective.

Maintaining an active lifestyle is a potent deterrent to osteoporosis, as is maintaining one's strength and balance throughout life. Taking a tumble at an advanced age is far more dangerous than taking a
spill in our younger years. Falls in later life are far more likely to result in hip fractures, head trauma, or even fatalities. Unfortunately,
Katharine Graham, publisher of the *Washington Post* and a vibrant
woman in her 80s, succumbed to head injuries suffered from a fall.
T'ai chi, an Eastern mind-body form of exercise, has been helpful in

developing balance skills and preventing falls in the elderly. It represents a graceful form of anti-aging medicine without a prescription.

Preventing Heart Disease

Before the onset of menopause, many women appear to be protected from coronary heart disease, heart attack, and stroke in comparison to men. It is not that unusual to hear of a man in his 40s having a heart attack and even dying after the first episode. Indeed, it is quite rare to hear of a woman who might have experienced a myocardial infarction before the age of menopause. It is as if Mother Nature has given us the gift of cardiac protection during our reproductive years.

Once the lease on our ovaries and reproductive capabilities has run out, our cardiac warranty expires as well. Now that women are living another 30-plus years after menopause, we are faced with the grim statistic that cardiovascular disease has become the leading cause of death in the postmenopausal age group. In 1984, the coronary death rate in women surpassed that of men. Most recently, the number of women dying each year from heart disease has jumped to over 370,000. In contrast, breast cancer claims just under 42,000 lives yearly.

Dr. Rose Marie Robertson, the president of the American Heart Association, wrote in a recent editorial of the journal *Circulation* that women show a "devastating lack of awareness, and don't believe heart disease can really affect them." She was referring to a survey showing that less than 10 percent of women believed heart disease was the greatest threat to their health, whereas 62 percent named cancer as the number one threat. In reality, if you include stroke under the umbrella of cardiovascular disease, then more than half a million women are victims. This represents double the number of cancer deaths in women and over 10 times the death rate from breast cancer. Although cancer is a scarier type of disease, heart disease and stroke are definitely becoming more preventable. Dr. Robertson is blunt in laying part of the blame on doctors who fail to educate their patients. However, it behooves all of us to become motivated and educate ourselves. Maximizing our health is the ultimate goal. Prevention is the weapon.

Prevention can take many forms. We should not be shocked to hear that lifestyle changes can make a difference. Exercise on a regular basis and with a regular goal of 30 minutes of aerobic (heart-rate accelerating) activity daily is ideal. If it can't be daily, aim for five or six days a week. Lowering cholesterol levels if they are high by modifying your diet, losing weight if necessary, or taking cholesterol-lowering drugs is also recommended. Recent studies have shown that the risk of heart disease could be reduced by 40 percent or more if cholesterol-lowering guidelines were followed.

Unfortunately, many women in particular assume they are not at risk and are more focused on the fears of developing cancer. However, women must be especially concerned about heart disease prevention because, once it develops, they do not recover as well as men. Statistically, a woman has a higher chance of dying than a man within one year of suffering a heart attack. She is also more likely to have a second heart attack in the following six years. Arriving at the emergency room may also be risky. Studies have unfortunately shown that women presenting with similar symptoms of chest pain and shortness of breath in an emergency room were less likely than men to be diagnosed promptly. Consequently, this resulted in further delays in receiving appropriate therapeutic measures such as blood thinners and beta-blocking drugs that can reduce stress on the heart and improve a patient's survival after a heart attack. Diagnostic procedures such as angiography were also delayed. What's a woman to do? To start with, become aware of your own risk parameters and be proactive. Knowledge is power. All women should be powerful players in their quest for optimum health.

Until very recently, the knight in shining armor to protect all menopausal women from untoward heart disease was estrogen. An overwhelming body of scientific research and literature showed that estrogen therapy protects a woman from heart attack by over 50 percent. This was a very impressive statistic and even cardiologists were labeling estrogen a woman's best friend. What has happened to change this?

Estrogen has been shown to decrease total cholesterol and LDL (low-density lipoprotein—the "bad" cholesterol) while increasing levels of HDL (high-density lipoprotein—the "good" cholesterol). These good-news statistics are still true. More recently, however, in the large multicenter Heart and Estrogen/Progestin Replacement Study (HERS), which included 2,763 women with existing heart disease (mean age 66.7 years), there was an increase in cardiovascular events after the first year of therapy. Surprisingly, when the statistics were further analyzed, after four to five years of hormone therapy, there was again some protection from recurrent heart problems in comparison to the placebo control group. This information has made the medical community amend the recommendation that estrogen therapy is always protective for all women against heart disease. If a woman has a history of preexisting heart disease, other options should be explored.

Recently, the prestigious American Heart Association, one of the most influential organizations in the field of heart disease prevention, recommended that women not start taking hormones simply to prevent heart trouble if there is a history of heart problems. However, those women taking hormones for the noncardiac benefits need not stop. Currently, a National Institutes of Health study of 27,500 women across the nation is investigating whether hormone replacement therapy should be used expressly to prevent cardiovascular disease. However, results are not expected for five more years.

Action Steps to Prevent Heart Disease

Barring any medical contraindication, the number one strategy is to incorporate regular physical activity into your daily (seven days a week) routine. Prioritizing physical activity becomes a lifelong health necessity rather than an item on the "if I have time" list. Don't shortchange yourself. As a busy physician with a full-time practice, and three active children, as well as a husband to manage, I used to feel guilty if I took personal time for exercise. Not any more. You owe it to yourself and your family—you'll be happier, healthier, and stronger. Numerous studies have shown that exercise is an excellent overall anti-aging strategy. Not only is this good for the heart and soul, but it benefits the bones, muscles, and mind as well.

Learning to reduce life's stresses will diminish high circulating levels of stress hormones in the blood. Some women experience rapid or irregular heartbeat during the perimenopausal to menopause transition. This can be related to hormonal fluctuations as well as anxiety or stress. Ways to lower stress include learning stress-management techniques; practicing meditation, yoga, or t'ai chi; adopting and loving a pet; volunteering for a worthwhile cause; taking up a fun and new hobby; listening to music; enjoying humor; and having at least two heavy doses of laughter a day. These steps should also translate into lower blood pressure levels. Try to achieve and maintain a healthy blood pressure, which optimally is less than 120/80 mm Hg.

Be aware of your overall diet and strive to keep total serum cholesterol less than 200 mg/dL, LDL less than 130 mg/dL, and HDL greater than or equal to 35 mg/dL. Adequate folic acid consumption may also be beneficial, as it lowers the risk of elevated homocysteine levels, another cardiovascular risk factor. Homocysteine is an amino acid, or protein building block, produced by the body typically as a byproduct of meat consumption. It can damage blood vessels and increase the risk of heart attack, stroke, and blood clots in the veins.

Prescription medications such as the statins (pravachol, simvastin, and atorvastatin) are very effective in lowering high cholesterol levels and reducing risk of cardiovascular disease. Alternatively, clinical trials in which subjects received an average daily intake of 47 grams/day of soy protein have shown a variable but significant decrease in total cholesterol, LDL cholesterol, and triglycerides. Soy milk products have become abundant in the markets and offer 6 to 8 grams of soy in an 8-ounce glass. Raloxifene, a selective estrogen receptor modulator (SERM), has also been shown to lower serum concentrations of total and LDL cholesterol, and may offer an option to traditional estrogen replacement.

Maintaining a desirable body weight and body mass index (BMI) is also important. A BMI of 25 to 29.9 is considered overweight, while a BMI of 30 or more is in the obese range. To calculate your BMI, take your weight in pounds and multiply by 704.5. Divide that number by your height in inches, squared. Recent research suggests that adults should try to maintain a BMI of between 18.5 and 21.9 for optimal health.

In a study conducted at Brigham and Women's Hospital and Harvard Medical School, overweight women, or those with a BMI of 25 to 29.9, were significantly more likely to develop gallstones, high blood pressure, high cholesterol, and heart disease. In addition, adults not traditionally considered to be overweight,—that is, those with BMI scores in the upper half of the healthy weight category (22 to 24.9)—were found to be at significantly greater risk of developing a chronic disease compared to the slimmer participants in the study. According to the NIH, having a BMI of 30 and above (about 30 pounds overweight) is considered obese.

In contrast to popular belief, menopause with or without estrogen replacement does not automatically lead to increased body weight. A combination of less overall activity, an anticipation or belief that weight gain always occurs at this time of life, and a lack of dietary modifications are the true culprits in perimenopausal/menopausal weight struggle.

Eating a healthful diet that is high in dietary fiber and low in total and saturated fats, cholesterol, and salt will fight obesity and improve cardiac health. This can be achieved by incorporating at least five servings of fresh fruits and vegetables daily and downsizing prepackaged snack foods and overall portion size. This mini-meal approach has worked well for my patients. By eating at regularly scheduled three- to four-hour intervals throughout the day, excessive hunger and subsequent overeating are avoided. Better and more consistent energy levels are also achieved.

Last but not least, make sure that your average overall calorie consumption on a daily basis is appropriate for your activity level as well as your body size. An occasional overindulgence is not a problem, it is a fact of life. However, consuming excessive calories on a regular basis will add up to excess pounds, guaranteed.

Be especially cautious about eating out. Typical restaurant portion sizes can be double or more of a day's total caloric needs. Be proactive when eating out. Split meals, ask for the dressing or sauce on the side, and skip heavy gravies altogether. Portion control and self-control go hand-in-hand, especially when there is conscious awareness and mindful eating. Practice these basic tips and you will be rewarded.

From Baby Boomer to Meno-Boomer: You've Come a Long Way, Baby!

We have moved beyond the Librium-laced menopause of our mothers' generation. Unlike the menopause of the silent 1950s, our generation has knowledge, power, science, research, and options. The good news is that we do indeed have choices—often multiple choices without an easy yes or no right answer. With options come decisions, and with decisions come responsibility for being our own best medical advocate.

But sometimes the information available to us can be overwhelming, somewhat confusing, and, at times, contradictory. Information that was held as gospel last week may suddenly be cast in new light with different medical interpretations and revamping of prior recommendations. Certainly fresh data is coming out on a daily basis, and it is not an easy task for either the health care provider or the patient to digest or comprehend it all.

Navigating Your Own Menopause

Ultimately we are the captain of our own vessel; we have the final say and the absolute responsibility for our own welfare. Certainly we can seek and receive advice, soak up words of wisdom, share experiences, and get caring, expert medical opinions. Whatever our decisions, whatever our options, they must be in harmony with our own beliefs.

It is estimated that only 30 percent of prescriptions written for estrogen replacement therapy for women in menopause are actually taken to the pharmacy and filled. What does this really mean? I don't believe that 70 percent of the women who don't follow through lose the prescriptions or even change their minds. I do believe that at the time the prescription is handed over to the woman by her physician, there is a lack of communication in at least 70 percent of these cases.

Whether consciously, subconsciously, or intuitively, a woman will arrive at her own decision. It has to resonate from within her. If a physician is not addressing her concerns adequately or answering questions satisfactorily, the prescription will not be filled. Even more important than whether or not the prescription was filled is the issue of whether or not the needs of the patient were met. Too often there is a gap between the health care provider and the health care receiver. Unfortunately, it is the patient who suffers the most. It is also the patient who will benefit the most by bridging this gap. I recommend getting the most from your medical appointment by being prepared.

How to Optimize Your Medical Appointment When Discussing the Estrogen Decision

1. Have as much information about your own family's health history as possible. Try to have the answers to the following health history questions in advance:

   a. Is there a history of heart disease or stroke?

b. Do any family members suffer from high cholesterol or high blood pressure?

c. If a relative has had a heart attack, at what age did it occur?

d. In particular, have any women suffered from heart disease or stroke?

e. Does cancer run in the family? What types and at what ages did they occur? In particular, are there any cancers of the female reproductive system, (breast, uterine, ovarian, cervical)?

f. Does osteoporosis or a family history of bone fractures exist?

2. Be up front about your own concerns and fears—be willing to address them even if the physician does not. By not addressing a hidden fear early on, you may sabotage your ability to have a positive response to therapy later on.

3. Specifically ask about side effects of any therapy, as well as the benefits.

4. Be direct with your question and ask your physician to explain the risk-benefit ratio of any therapy. Ask about the risks of not choosing a particular therapy. Be sure to ask about options or alternatives. Discuss the potential benefits of soy products, phytoestrogens, and vitamin E as complementary supplements.

5. Always check that you are starting on the smallest effective dose. When it comes to hormone replacement therapy, less appears to be better.

6. Ask about forms of herbal remedies or any type of complementary medicine that you are trying. Even if a product is not prescribed, there is a possibility of a potential interaction and your physician should be aware of this. This will also put your own mind at ease that what you are doing is in harmony with your physician's recommendations.

7. Be open about your own beliefs and share them with your physician so there is greater understanding between you. For example, if you are dead set against hormone replacement therapy, let your physician know so he or she can work with you in exploring other options. If your physician is not aware that you hold a strong belief, it is harder to forge a partnership or develop trust. In the end it is your health and happiness that are at stake.

8. Communication is at least a 50-50 proposition. Take responsibility for your half. If you are having problems, concerns, or misgivings about a particular form of therapy, don't be a dropout—call and discuss the situation. If your physician is not responsive to your concerns, find one who will be.

Now that you have mastered handling your own midlife transition, find out how you can help your mate navigate his midlife challenges.

CHAPTER 3

Andropause: The Male Change

While it is universally accepted that puberty is a physiological and psychological phenomenon affecting both sexes, the question "Does male midlife transition exist?" is about as valid as "Does male puberty exist?" Until now, this segment of the male life cycle has been poorly understood, and practically ignored despite the significant impact on men's lives and the women they live with. One can only speculate that perhaps a touch of male denial in the predominantly male medical community might have contributed to the undercurrent of controversy that exists even today as to the validity of a male climacteric. Surveys have shown a significantly higher acceptance of the concept of a male menopause among female physicians than their male counterparts.

Granted, male and female menopauses are not equivalent conditions. However, by allowing themselves to accept the notion of a male andropause as universally as they accept female menopause, couples can leave the dark ages of hormonal ignorance. When it comes to hormones, ignorance definitely is not bliss; it is a disaster waiting to happen.

Part of the controversy in acknowledging male menopause is the lack of a definitive physiological landmark, as in the cessation of menses for women. However, even for women, the changes that occur in our minds and bodies leading up to the end of menses do so gradually over months and even years. This perimenopausal period in women can be frustrating and at times difficult to diagnose because of the irregularities in mood, energy levels, memory, menses, and other physical changes. So, too, for men at midlife—except they lack the menstrual cycle clues to guide them through their periandropausal journey. Lucky for us women that we have the external hormonal monitor vis-à-vis menses. Now if we can only enlighten the other half of the human species.

The terms *male menopause, viropause, andropause, male climacteric,* and more recently the acronym *ADAM* (androgen decline in the aging male) have all been used in the medical literature. Just as with the condition itself, there does not seem to be a consensus as to the most appropriate terminology.

However, even more important than labeling is recognizing the common signs and symptoms. Male menopause is not a disease but the gradual changes that occur physically and emotionally, typically between ages 40 and 60. It is *not* defined by the occurrence of a midlife crisis—"You'll know you've hit male menopause when you've had your first midlife crisis" doesn't apply here. However, it is certainly beneficial to recognize signs and symptoms before a crisis brews. If you can imagine the impact of 220 million baby boomers simultaneously having one worldwide midlife crisis, the combustion alone might threaten the existence of the human species. Many conflicts and wars were directly influenced by midlife-induced male saber rattling.

When Men Suffer in Silence

There can be subtle, and perhaps not so subtle, physical, emotional, and sometimes "difficult to get a handle on it" type of changes.

Forty-nine-year-old Barry appeared to have everything in the world to be grateful for: a lovely home, a beautiful wife, three healthy kids—two already in college—and a profitable company that he was contemplating selling. What was brewing inside Barry's body and mind was a completely different picture.

For two years Barry just hadn't felt like himself. True, there was a lot to be happy for—but it didn't seem to register. Instead, Barry was looking for the next jolt of excitement to give him back his energy, his enthusiasm, and maybe even his old eyesight. Even little things bothered him. Besides the inconvenience of wearing glasses, he hated the graying hair, the lack of energy, the loss of excitement for things he used to love, and especially the slowing of his sex life. He hated to admit that he couldn't play tennis the way he used to—the endurance just wasn't there. The worst part—and this was new—was getting up at night to urinate, and having an embarrassingly weak stream. His wife was going through her "perimenopause thing." He felt there was no one he could turn to—besides, men don't talk, they bottle up.

Barry was fortunate to have a wife who gently persuaded him to have a physical exam—it had been over five years since his last one—and he was willing to invite his wife along. Although he wasn't ill, Barry knew he was definitely not himself. A full physical exam was performed and blood work drawn. Nothing unusual or dangerous seemed to be going on. It was not until the next visit, when Barry sat down with his doctor, that the true situation was revealed.

After a more candid discussion and a review of the lab results, Barry learned he was experiencing a mild depression, some low thyroid levels, an enlarged prostate, and some borderline declines in his testosterone levels. Getting checked was definitely the right thing to do. Barry was able to begin some low-dose hormone therapy, strength training, and an adjustment in his diet. His mood and energy levels improved, and he was relieved to know that an ultrasound showed the prostate enlargement was benign. By cutting back on his fluid and alcohol intake before bedtime, he was even able to sleep through the night. When he did urinate first thing in the morning, it was full force.

One Man's Affair: A Sign of Inner Despair

Curt, a 52-year-old corporate executive, was not as lucky as Barry. Blaming work pressure, Curt tried to ignore his increasing bouts of insomnia and irritability. He kept feeling anxious and he took his frustrations out on those closest to him, including Cecile, his wife of 25 years, and their daughter, Samantha. Perhaps if Curt had known that the manifestations of male menopause could be subtle and variable yet include a host of symptoms such as anxiety, irritability, fatigue, depression, decreased libido, erectile dysfunction, and changes in mood, he would have sought help. Instead he withdrew from his family and sought refuge in an impulsive affair that shattered his domestic life and catapulted him into greater depression.

Only after the breakup of his marriage and the ending of the affair did he seek counseling. Curt learned that he was not the only man to have these types of feelings at this time of life. It was much more common than he would have ever imagined—only most men don't share these feelings. The therapist referred him to a physician who was tuned in to the physical and emotional challenges of midlife men. After a careful and thorough history and physical exam, he was able to treat Curt's insomnia. With his sleep restored, Curt felt like he had a new lease on life—his energy levels improved, his irritability and anxiety diminished, and he was able to take a more realistic and hard look at where his life was going. He started to invest the time and energy needed to restore himself physically and emotionally.

By committing himself to a regular exercise regime, a healthier diet, and time set aside for life-enhancing activities, such as listening to his favorite operas, reading for enjoyment, and meditating, Curt turned his life around. Unfortunately, the damage to his marriage was irreparable. Curt's advice to other men experiencing similar problems: "Don't be a fool like me. You're not the only one out there going through these things. Get help, seek advice early—don't wait until it's too late; you won't always get a second chance."

How Do I Know If I'm Experiencing Male Menopause?

The following survey will give you better insight into your midlife status. Please answer yes or no.

1. I have difficulty getting and sustaining an erection.
2. I have fewer morning erections than I did when I was 30 years old.
3. My energy levels are lower than they were at age 30.
4. My endurance is less than I would like.
5. I frequently feel irritable and/or anxious.
6. I feel or have been told that I look/act as if I'm depressed.
7. I have trouble falling or staying asleep.
8. I get warm or hot "flash" sensations.
9. I feel my libido is decreasing.
10. It takes me longer to recover from physical activities.
11. I have more mood swings or emotional fluctuations than I used to.
12. I have frequent concerns about my virility.
13. It takes me longer to recover from illness.
14. I have noticed less muscle and more flab in the last five years.
15. I frequently feel that time is running out.

Multiply every yes response by 5 and every no response by 1. If the answer to question 1 is yes, add 15 more points. Subtract your no totals from your yes totals; if there are only no responses, just report your total. If your score is 40 or greater, midlife changes may be taking a toll on your physical and emotional well-being. Scores between 29 and 40 are borderline—be aware of subtle and not so subtle changes. Scores of 15 or less indicate that you are not exhibiting the more common signs and symptoms of male menopause.

Bill Clinton: Poster Boy for Male Midlife Crisis?

Perhaps the Monica Lewinsky–Bill Clinton scandal represents the most internationally publicized example of male midlife lapse of judgment in recent time. Having a past history of infidelity does not soften the outrageous and risky nature of Bill Clinton's behavior. After all, the man was intelligent enough to be at Oxford and savvy enough to be elected president. One has to ask, "Whatever was going on in his brain?" His actions were risky not only for himself but for the integrity of the presidential office and the nation for that matter. Was there a compromise in the blood flow to his brain causing such incredibly risky behavior? Most likely not—a compromise in blood flow would represent cerebral insufficiency and cause signs and symptoms of a stroke. The president didn't appear to exhibit any residual signs of a stroke.

It has been speculated that hormones played a role. Certainly if Hillary is willing to forgive and forget, than the rest of us should follow suit. Although with time the hoopla and intense notoriety will simmer down, the significance of this very public example of a 50-something couple working through their menopause moments should not be forgotten: he winding down from the top of his political career, while she aspiring to new heights in her political quests, each accepting the other's decision and status. And yes, they certainly experienced their own roller-coaster and double-menopause moments. Although the behind-the-scenes discussions, fights, and healing process rightly remain hidden from public view, there are many couples looking for answers to their own dilemmas and asking, "What do we do now?"

Action Steps for Men

What is the next step if it looks like you're a candidate for male menopause poster boy of the year? First, let me congratulate you for taking the bold step of honestly facing the issues and taking the bull by the horns. Self-awareness is the key to self-help and rejuvenation. Take note if you are experiencing both physical and emotional symptoms, emotional symptoms alone, or just physical symptoms. Typically, andropause encompasses both the physical and emotional elements. If there are no physical symptoms at all, and you are not certain about any subtle emotional changes, this is a good opportunity to check in with your significant other about changes you might not be aware of.

If you are aware of these changes, take comfort in knowing that you are not alone. According to Census Bureau projections, the number of men in the United States between the ages of 40 and 55 will be close to 60 million by 2020. Fortunately, progress is being made in the field of male hormone research, although we are currently at least 30 years behind the level of knowledge we currently have for female menopause. This doesn't mean we should ignore the problems, stick our heads in the sand, and pretend there is no such thing as male midlife transition or ADAM. The true dilemma is that there are no set guidelines.

Start with a Medical Checkup

Unfortunately, according to a survey by the Commonwealth Fund, American men are out of touch with the health care system and their own health. In a study based on a Louis Harris and Associates poll of 1,500 men and 2,850 women taken between May and November 1998, one-third of the men did not have a regular doctor to go to for medical advice. This finding is consistent with the observation that men seek health care less frequently than women. As summed up by Drs. Danielle Nahon and Nedra Lander, two psychologists of the first men's clinic in North America, "The male gender role stereotype demands that men be healthy, strong and self-sufficient. Society teaches men to ignore physical symptoms that may be associated with the onset of illness." Men, this is not the time to be the strong and silent type. You can still be strong, but don't remain silent or invisible. A general physical screening and health exam are a good start. Women undergo annual exams and take better preventive health measures than men. At a minimum, men should be screened for heart disease, colon cancer, diabetes, and other medical conditions based upon the physical exam and family history. Even male pattern baldness—especially balding at the crown of the head—and a pot- or beer belly may be a warning sign of heart disease. Get a checkup—you may be at risk for more than vanity alone.

Measure Total and Free Levels of Blood Testosterone

The most accurate assessment of testosterone levels is a morning blood sample. Testosterone levels peak in the morning. Keep in mind that testosterone is a sex steroid hormone and that it is carried in the blood by SHBG (sex hormone–binding globulin). Because it is possible to have a normal total testosterone level and still be testosterone deficient, a more accurate assessment is to measure the amount of testosterone that is free in the bloodstream and that is not bound to SHBG. Your physician should therefore measure free testosterone as well.

Muscle mass, strength, and bone mass diminish with both age and lower testosterone levels. On the other hand, fat mass and erectile dysfunction increase and, not surprisingly, one's sense of well-being can parallel the decline in this hormone level.

Have a Prostate Screening and Check PSA (Prostate-Specific Antigen) Levels

Make sure you are screened for cancer of the prostate. Approximately 37,000 men die annually with this cancer, and another 180,000 men are newly diagnosed each year. Occult prostate cancers are detectable in approximately 25 percent of men under age 40. All men 40 years of age or older need a yearly prostate checkup. This should include a digital rectal exam to assess the size of the prostate as well as a highly sensitive blood test that measures minute quantities of a protein called prostate-specific antigen, or PSA. If the PSA level is too high, the risk of a hidden prostate cancer increases. An abnormal PSA blood test and/or any suspicious signs or symptoms should be followed up by further studies (ultrasound, MRI, biopsy, etc.).

Get a Tune-Up

After a certain amount of mileage, anticipate that a tune-up is in order. It's time, especially if you haven't done so already, to evaluate what will keep the parts running smoothly and efficiently for the long haul. Why let yourself turn into a jalopy when you really want to be a Lamborghini? The best advice: stay as fit and active as is medically permitted and eat foods that are in synchrony with healthy living. Stick with premium low-fat, lower calorie, higher nutrient fare; avoid fast food, fried food, and artery-clogging sludge. Be a Lamborghini . . . and treat yourself like one.

Monitor the Happiness Factor

Take an inventory of what makes you happy on a day-to-day basis, including people, things, events, hobbies, sports, work, volunteerism, future goals—whatever it takes. If your list is shorter than ten, you need to have an emergency restocking of your happiness storage chest. We grow old not just by the number of years, but by losing our ideals, our dreams, and our capacity to be happy. Sometimes our receptors for happiness become tarnished, leading to depression, irritability, and anger. There can be physical as well as emotional causes. Assessing this sensitive topic with your significant other might provide insight; it might also be wise to consult with your physician or therapist.

What If I Do Have Low Testosterone Levels?

Take comfort, you are not alone. Circulating levels of free, biologically available testosterone decrease by as much as 50 percent in men between the ages of 25 and 75, while one out of two men over the age of 50 is considered to be in a low testosterone state. Normal levels are between 270 and 1,200 ng/mL. Aging as well as heredity may play a significant role in the progressive decline in male hormone. Other contributory factors include a history of testicular trauma, orchitis, or the presence of obesity. Lifestyle factors also play a role, including that ubiquitous *S* word *stress*—both physical and psychological. Male triathletes have lower blood testosterone levels after a race than at the start line. Excess alcohol will also contribute negatively.

What about mood? Some studies have shown significant improvement in symptoms of depression, irritability, anger, sense of well-being, and enhanced energy when treated with male hormone. Other well-controlled scientific studies have also shown that testosterone supplements increase muscle mass and strength and improved libido and erectile dysfunction in two-thirds of cases. Male sexuality as well as testosterone supplementation are discussed in greater depth in Chapter 5, "Midlife Sexuality: The Male Perspective."

What Precipitates the Male Midlife Crisis?

Andrew and Helen had been married for 28 years. With four grown children, a handsome financial situation, and plenty of friends, they were enjoying their midlife status. Both 53, and both in very good health, they were looking forward to celebrating their twenty-eighth anniversary in Hawaii. According to Helen, Andrew "turned into someone else" after they landed in Maui.

Ed had been a very good friend of Andrew's. Fifty-six-year-old Ed was a golfing buddy as well as a business associate. It was a shock to everyone when Ed developed colon cancer. He looked healthy on the outside: fit, trim, and energetic. But the surgery, chemotherapy and hospitalizations took their toll. It was unacceptable that this healthy specimen of a man, in his absolute prime, would succumb to a disease that is curable when detected early. Ed's death six months earlier left Andrew with a scar so deep he could not see or feel it until it worked its way to the surface. With a twist of psychological irony, the change of environment to the relaxing atmosphere of Hawaii unleashed all these pent-up feelings and the scar erupted.

Neither Helen nor Andrew was prepared. Somehow, being on vacation in Hawaii and being able to enjoy his life while his dear friend Ed was no longer alive seemed to push Andrew into a new frame of mind. It hit him like a ton of bricks: he was no longer immortal. If it could happen to Ed, it could happen to anyone, he felt. Helen tried to reason with him: "No one is immortal; nothing has changed with our health. We'll make sure to get all the right checkups."

After their return home, Andrew continued to drift. If he wasn't in his moody state, he would go into his daredevil mode—he fluctuated between depression and recklessness. Never having even desired a motorcycle, he bought one and took it out for long rides on remote windy roads. It was almost as if he wanted to confront death before death confronted him. When Helen was finally able to get him to seek help, for her sake, he discovered he had a delayed, and dramatic, reaction to Ed's death. With some therapy, he was able to accept his vulnerabilities and calm down to a more normal and safer lifestyle.

Common Causes of Male Midlife Crisis

Loss or Downsizing of a Job

A man's sense of identity is often tied to what he does rather than who he is. When women and men are both asked to complete the sentence "I am a _____," women more often than not respond "a mother" or "a wife" even if they are professionals or employed outside of the home. Men will answer with their occupation first and foremost. So it is not surprising that when a man loses this overwhelming part of his identity, especially if it is usurped by a younger man or woman, this can tilt the balance from stable to fragile. A man's sense of masculinity can be challenged by the loss of his job. A primary social network may also be lost, as many men do not develop personal relationships outside of the workplace. Similarly, retirement, even though voluntary, can also trigger changes in perception of self and masculine identity, especially if the man has not developed or cultivated interests outside of his work.

Separation and/or Divorce

The identity of being a married man with all the trimmings of that stable role is shattered by separation or divorce. In a sense, the man is now free to be looked upon as uncommitted and available, a state that he may have not experienced for decades. This may result in a sense of new identity and, not surprisingly, new behaviors. Some scientists have even speculated that a newly divorced man who is on the hunt for a partner may actually experience surges in blood testosterone levels.

Children Leaving Home

Another stimulus to the male midlife crisis is the event of children leaving the nest. Whether to go to college or to go off and make their own mark on the world, when children jump ship there is an immediate rocking of the boat. For some couples, this is a long-anticipated and joyful occasion. For others, the event signals aging, no longer being needed to care for young and dependent children, and a time to reevaluate or question one's priorities in life.

Sometimes the act of a child leaving home will trigger a mirror need in a man who has an underlying desire to leave home as well. Now it can be rationalized that the kids are grown and no longer dependent on Dad for everything in their life. Now it's Dad's turn to spread his wings as well. Such was the case for 51-year-old Marvin, who announced to Barb, his wife of 30 years, that he was leaving home to explore his options in the world. The timing couldn't have been more perfect; his son Jeff had just left for college the week before and Barb had noted that Marvin was becoming increasingly anxious. Having received a two-month sabbatical from his high-paying job, Marvin gave Barb 24 hours' notice and left for paths unknown. Failing to persuade him not to leave, Barb filed for divorce and blamed it on hormones or midlife crisis. Still perplexed five years later, Barb wonders if either of them could have done anything differently. She is now happily remarried to a man she feels has "better insight into his inner self."

Experiencing Erectile Failure Twice in a Row

An occasional problem with an erection can be a common occurrence and easily explained by reasons of fatigue, a bit too much alcohol consumption, a stressful day, or just not being in the mood. But to a midlife man who is already sensitive to the hallmarks of aging, such as the annoyance of wearing reading glasses, the appearance of a progressively receding hairline, and an advancing waistline, the threat of becoming impotent may be just enough to push him over the edge.

Sixty-year-old Howard was not amused when his wife, Phoebe, began to affectionately refer to his erection problems as "that *limpido* thing." He was not pleased by the situation nor his wife's casual and humorous approach. To prove himself, he decided to see if his plumbing would work with a younger female specimen. His secretary, a 28-year-old single woman, was available and desirous of the attentions of an older man. She was also a quick but temporary solution to Howard's "limpido" problem. By the time the affair ended, so had Phoebe and Howard's marriage.

Becoming a Grandparent

For the man who is fighting mortality, becoming a grandfather can trigger distinct feelings of discomfort. The image of Gramps may bring back memories of his own grandparents' fragility and feebleness. Trying to maintain a more youthful image, some grandfatherly males try to prove their virility and studsmanship by becoming a new papa at a ripe old age.

This seems to be almost standard behavior for certain celebrity males. Affectionately referred to as "dinosaur dads," this growing list includes the following dads and the age they sired their offspring: Woody Allen (63), Larry King (65), Jack Nicholson (53, 55), Anthony Quinn (79, 81), Saul Bellow (83), Tony Randall (77, 78), and Warren Beatty (55, 57, 60). It is far more socially acceptable for an older man to marry a younger woman than the other way around. This is a trend that appears to be on the upswing, and not just for celebrities. Perhaps the antidote to psychological aging for some men is to actively revert back to new parenthood rather than passively succumb to grandparenthood. Reproducing with a younger partner can bolster some men's sense of youthfulness and prove their virility.

A Health Crisis

Nothing snaps the reality of mortality into view more than the loss of one's health or the fear of impending death. Such a situation can jolt a man from his day-to-day life. A new path to follow, a new quest, or a spiritual journey often becomes paramount. Hard-driving Mayor Rudy Giuliani of New York abandoned his political aspirations of becoming a New York senator after learning that he had cancer of the prostate.

Besides dropping out of his heated political campaign, he publicly announced that he was divorcing his wife (failing to inform her first), and professed his intentions of becoming a better person, all in the course of one week. Perhaps referring to this episode as a midlife crisis is an understatement. As one New York cabbie was quoted as saying, "Giuliani was having the 'Big Mac' of midlife crises." Well stated.

Death or Illness of a Peer

Life is short and transient—this is the message that hits a man between the eyes when a peer succumbs to illness. The immediate thought is, "It could have been me." For men accustomed to power and fantasies of immortality, the thought of personal mortality is shocking and humbling. Although women score higher on tests of death anxiety than men, women are more open about their fears, since men deny or minimize their anxieties, including fears of death. The fact that women bear children and bring life into the world can provide a personal link to immortality in the light of death, whereas the man cannot directly procreate. The death or illness of a close peer is a much louder wake-up call for a man in denial of his own immortality, and for that matter, his own midlife transition.

Deal with Denial

Denial is to midlife development as reckless driving is to adolescent survival. Denial, in essence, is an anti-coping and self-limiting mechanism that compounds in the midlife years. We are at a crossroads in the world of preventive medicine and the field of anti-aging medicine. While baby boomers lust over newly hyped products that promise to erase years from their face (or other body part) or add years to their life expectancy, on an individual basis, men are the least likely to admit they are entering a new phase of their life. While women have concrete evidence of menopause (the end of their menses), men are faced with an ill-defined collection of symptoms that may not ring a bell that they, too, are facing hormone changes with physical and emotional consequences.

In a study that included over 300 male veterans, doctors found that 89 percent of them admitted they had symptoms that they believed were synonymous with andropause. The majority reported onset between the ages of 50 and 60 years. However, individually these men did not seek help as they were not aware that such an entity as andropause even existed. One might wonder why not.

Perhaps the explanation can be found in the current attitude of the medical community—the male medical community in particular. As a female physician specializing in hormonal issues, I am asked to lecture throughout the country to groups of health care providers (physicians, nurses, physician assistants, nurse practitioners, and the like). When I begin my lecture I ask for an informal show of hands as to how many in the audience believe that women go through menopause. The response is typically a universal show of hands. When I ask the audience how many believe that men also can go through a change of life, albeit somewhat different from a woman's, nearly all the women raise their hands while the men in the room typically look stone-faced and sit on their hands.

Talk about denial—and these are our medical brethren. There is good news though—these men are willing to listen and to learn. At the end of the lecture, after presenting and discussing the scientific data and the most current medical literature, I take a new poll and there are far more male physicians raising their hands agreeing that yes, indeed, male andropause does exist. All it takes is a few good men and women to spread the word and make the medical community more aware of this common condition. After male physicians become aware, they can then help their male patients who are suffering in silence or otherwise.

For Women: How Can You Help Your Man?

After working with so many of my female patients to understand and cope with the myriad of challenges facing them during their midlife transition, I am frequently asked, "What can I do to help my husband with his change of life?" The answer is simple: "Nothing!" Now don't panic. We all want to help our dearly beloved—especially if he is driving us crazy with his attitude or behavior. Let me expand on what "nothing" actually means.

As an example, let's use the medical profession's Hippocratic Oath commanding all doctors to "Above all, do no harm." Similarly, all women seeking to help their mate sail through his own midlife adjustment must take the following oath: "Above all, do nothing that is threatening." Do not whine, cajole, command, or demand that he do something about his problem. Lead by support, love, and example. And most importantly, acknowledge that his changes are part of a normal process that *all* men go through. Many normal and progressive men are getting help checking out and fixing what needs to be fixed. Many men are scared to admit, even to themselves, that they are experiencing changes. This can lead to irritability and emotional withdrawal. And this is where your skill is needed.

The Quiet Voice of Reason

Don was thrilled to be in early retirement. For 10 years his growing business had demanded lots of travel—so much travel that being away from home was routine. Don used to joke that he knew he had been away too long when he would be in his own bed, pick up the phone, and ask for a morning wake-up call. But now, that was behind him. Having sold his business, Don and his 50-year-old wife, Amy, were fortunate to have their health and the financial resources to enjoy their new freedom. But something was missing.

Amy had been looking forward to the time when she and Don could spend more time together, pursue hobbies, and do more traveling together. This had been both of their dreams. However, reality wasn't going that way. Don was restless and didn't have the social resources that Amy had developed. In fact, he hardly knew anyone in their own neighborhood. Amy felt guilty leaving Don at home while she played bridge with friends or volunteered at the hospital. Don's unhappiness took its toll on both of them. His drinking increased while her desire to leave the house escalated. Instead of enjoying each other more, each was secretly blaming the other for their own unhappiness—until a light came on in Amy's head.

Rather than pretend that there were no problems, and mindful of not laying blame, Amy came up with a plan. One evening she took Don out on a surprise date. She had made the dinner reservations, planned which movie to go to, and even had a special dessert treat waiting at home to top the night off with. The surprise date was such a success that they decided to take turns weekly preparing surprises for each other. Knowing that Don was not prepared for the dramatic change in his lifestyle made Amy more sympathetic and supportive. She acknowledged her own anger and used it to become proactive rather than resentful.

Contrast this approach to that of Tom and Angela. Sixty-three-year-old Tom had also recently retired but had a hobby lined up. An avid golfer, he had always wanted to have the luxury of playing several times a week. Angela, a 52-year-old retired elementary school teacher, also had just retired at Tom's urging. She loved teaching and felt she could have continued for at least five more years, as she was actively involved in the mentoring of younger teachers. Nonetheless, Angela was grateful that this was a time of life for both of them to reconnect. The problem here was that Tom was looking forward to golf and the comfort that his wife would be free from work.

Angela soon felt neglected and missed the rewards of being appreciated at her school. Rather than drawing them closer, the retirement years pushed them into separate corners. Angela became bitter and resentful. Tom turned more to golf. It took a mutual friend to suggest that they each could pursue their own interests and schedule together time as well. Angela went back to work part-time and recaptured her true spirit that was so sorely missed. Tom discovered he could enjoy free time even while his wife was professionally occupied. With these adjustments they each discovered they could cherish the other even more.

Be tuned into each other's needs and willing to talk. Silence is deadly, not golden—especially at midlife. Holding secret grudges, fears, or keeping one's true desires hidden will eventually wear down the spirit. Pretending to maintain the status quo when the ship is slowly sinking sabotages success. Getting your man to open up can be particularly challenging, but it helps to let him know all men go through midlife changes and do better when they confront the changes. Make dates to exercise together, and take up new hobbies that you can enjoy together, such as bridge, social dancing, photography, adult education classes, book discussion clubs, live theater shows, and dinners out. Exercise the mind and the body—make yourself irresistible and become enchanting to each other again.

And don't overlook friendships. A male may feel isolated, especially after retirement if most of his social interactions with other men occurred at the office. Go out with other couples and keep in mind potential matches for your mate. What are your friend's husband's interests? Perhaps the two men could become tennis partners. It is often easier for the wives to break the ice and make the introductions. Join organizations that might offer stimulating or rewarding activities for both of you. This certainly could include philanthropic work as well.

How we approach our later years and the zest we bring with us will make all the difference in the world. Think positively, act positively, and hook up with like-minded folks. If you can't find a club, consider organizing one. Positive attitudes can be just as contagious as negative ones. Men are regarding their later years as an opportunity to participate in activities that interest them or are rewarding in ways other than financially. Mentoring younger men or boys may help develop a man's spiritual side and provide relief from focusing on competitive endeavors. Being appreciated for one's wisdom or experience can help restore a sense of purpose and fulfillment for a man who feels left behind.

PART II

Dealing with Your Partner's Hormones

CHAPTER 4

Midlife Sexuality:
The Female Perspective

For many women, the life events of perimenopause and menopause usher in a major downshift in sexual function. Symptoms of loss of desire, painful intercourse, diminished sexual activity, and blunted sexual responsiveness are often kept in the closet or ignored in comparison to other change-of-life events. As far as sexuality is concerned, a policy of "don't ask, don't tell" is frequently encountered in the traditional medical setting.

Health care providers typically lack adequate training in taking a sexual history and may feel intimidated by the subject. Likewise, the patient may feel that the issue of sex is not significant enough to take up the doctor's time—especially if the doctor is not even asking. Hence the cycle persists and becomes compounded if the woman's partner might be experiencing sexual problems at this time of life as well. These changes in sexual function are often not even recognized as being associated with the hormonal decline of menopause or andropause and can result in significant dissatisfaction between mid-life couples. In about one-third of couples, male sexual dysfunction contributes to decreased frequency of intercourse, while the remaining two-thirds of couples are affected by menopausal physiology.

Neither husband nor wife is happy with the way their lives are going, yet they are unable to communicate their feelings.

In addition to concerns about osteoporosis, heart disease, stroke, and mental function, many menopausal women do worry about sexuality and the loss of libido. Attention to female sexual dissatisfaction during menopause has increased due to the sheer numbers of female baby boomers entering their 50s. Women are also becoming more vocal about their sexual concerns and are seeking solutions.

In a survey conducted by internationally renowned gynecologists Drs. Phil Sarrel and Malcolm Whitehead, it was found that 86 percent of the women attending a London menopause clinic reported the presence of sexual problems. Loss of sexual desire and vaginal dryness were at the top of the list. The situation is aggravated when the partner is also experiencing changes or difficulties at the same time and neither has a clue about the effects of midlife physiology. For a midlife man, starting an affair with a younger woman is more often about seeking reassurance for his potency—a form of self-medication or hormonal boost—than about establishing a new relationship. A midlife woman may also experience unmet needs— typically more of the emotional kind, but sexual dissatisfaction can play a role as well. Women are becoming more tuned in to their sexual responses and seeking help for these concerns. Unfortunately, not all physicians may inquire about this aspect of our lives during a routine office visit, so as women we have to become the responsible parties in being proactive.

In one of the largest studies ever conducted in the United States of the over-45 population, close to 1,400 adults were surveyed in 1999 by the AARP/*Modern Maturity* on factors affecting sexual attitudes, activities, and satisfaction as well as behavior and lifestyles. According to Constance Swank, research director at AARP, "We found that a majority of mid-life and older adults feel good about their lives right now, and 67 percent of men and 57 percent of women say a satisfying sexual relationship is important to that quality of life." When asked what would improve their sexual satisfaction, the top four responses for the men were better health for themselves followed by better health for their partners, less stress, and more free time. For the women, the four key ingredients for enhancing sexual satisfaction were less stress, better health for their partners, better health for themselves, and finding a partner.

What Marsha Didn't Know

A woman's perception of her body is an important component of her sexual health. Although 55-year-old Marsha took excellent care of herself by eating well, exercising aerobically three to four times a week, and weight training twice a week, she became upset when her naked body no longer caused her husband, Sam, to have an erection. She acknowledged that she certainly didn't look like her 21-year-old self, but she also knew that she looked and felt younger than many women her age. As time went on, she became depressed over the situation and felt she was no longer woman enough to keep her mate excited. Finally forcing herself to discuss the situation with her own physician, Marsha discovered that her husband was showing the natural changes in male sexual response with age. Visual stimulation alone is not enough to stimulate an erection in many men over 50 and it takes more direct manual or oral stimulation to accomplish erections.

This was obviously more about nature and Sam's andropause than Marsha's own menopausal changes. However, like many women in her situation, she felt it was her appearance that had caused the lack of immediate response and blamed herself. Her own frustration had turned to anger and then depression. Fortunately for both Sam and Marsha, learning about the normal changes a man goes through and making some adjustments in their usual sexual routine helped save their marriage.

Sexual Awareness: It's Never Too Late

Many women remain sexually active well into their 80s. However, age-related changes can have a direct as well as indirect impact on midlife sexuality. Some surveys suggest that sexual dissatisfaction occurs in over 30 percent of women greater than 45 years of age. How would you rate your level of sexual satisfaction?

Midlife Sexuality Quiz

The following quiz is designed to help you determine if there are areas in your sex life that have changed because of aging or hormonal transition. For items 1–10, please answer yes or no.

1. Are you 45 years of age or older?
2. Have you had a hysterectomy, with removal of the ovaries, within the last two years?
3. Are you taking birth control pills?
4. Do you use hormone replacement therapy?
5. Do you use estrogen?
6. Do you use testosterone?
7. Do you use progesterone or progestion?
8. Do you have difficulty getting a good night's sleep in general?
9. Do you and your partner generally go to bed at different times?
10. Is intercourse more uncomfortable now than it was 6 to 12 months ago?

For items 11–20, please choose the best response.

11. In the past six months, my desire for sex has been:
    a. High
    b. Moderate
    c. Low

12. In the past six months, lubrication (becoming "wet") before or during sex has been:
    a. Improved
    b. Unchanged
    c. Reduced

13. In the past six months, how often has sexual activity led to orgasms (climax)?
    a. Most of the time
    b. Half the time
    c. Infrequently
    d. Not at all

14. In the past six months, have you felt emotionally close with your partner during sexual activity?
    a. Most of the time
    b. Half the time
    c. Infrequently
    d. Not at all

15. Over the past six months, what has been your degree of satisfaction with your sex life?
    a. Very satisfying
    b. Somewhat satisfying
    c. Somewhat dissatisfying
    d. Very unsatisfying

16. Over the past six months, what has been your sense of satisfaction with your physical self?
    a. Completely satisfied
    b. Could use some improvement
    c. Room for much improvement
    d. I'm so disappointed, I don't want to discuss it.
    e. It doesn't matter to me.

17. Over the past six months, what has been your sense of satisfaction with your partner's physical self?

  a. Completely satisfied

  b. Could use some improvement

  c. Room for much improvement

  d. I'm so disappointed, I don't want to discuss it.

  e. It doesn't matter to me.

18. Over the past six months, what has been the state of your emotional or inner self?

  a. Stable

  b. Peaceful

  c. Unpredictable, volatile

  d. Needs some assistance

  e. I'm not in touch with my inner self.

19. Over the past six months, what do you think has been the state of your partner's emotional or inner self?

  a. Stable

  b. Peaceful

  c. Unpredictable, volatile

  d. Needs some assistance

  e. I'm not tuned in to his/her inner being.

20. Overall, how satisfied are you with your current sexual relationship with your partner?

  a. Completely satisfied

  b. Could use some improvement

  c. Room for much improvement

  d. I'm so disappointed, I don't want to discuss it.

  e. It doesn't matter to me.

SCORES

For questions 1–10:   Four or more yes answers—your midlife
sexuality could benefit from strategic
planning.

For questions 11–20:   Five or more c, d, or e answers—your sex life
is overdue for a tune-up.
Seven or more a answers—you and your
partner are definitely doing something right.
Seven or more b answers—watch out, your
sex life may be going through a transition.

Sexual function issues are, like sexuality itself, highly personal. Menopause may bring about certain physical and emotional changes common to all women, but specific variables can have an additional impact. How a woman perceives the process of aging, whether or not she is on hormone replacement therapy, the presence or absence of relationship issues, in addition to cultural issues all play a significant role. Psychological barriers, previous sexual functioning, as well as her general medical well-being will affect her sexuality as well. Problems arise mainly when we are not up front with ourselves or fail to communicate with our partner. If there are difficulties, pretending everything is okay or trying to maintain the status quo perpetuates the problem. It becomes part of our invisible baggage that we respond to in different ways.

There is no question that marital problems are one of the most common causes of a decline in sexual activity. Conversely, loss of sexual relations can lead to an increase in marital discord. For some women, chronic problems in the marital relationship can lead to built-up resentment toward the spouse. With the advent of menopause, they feel they now have permission to decline sex. So, too, for women who did not find sex pleasurable before the change of life. These women may look forward to ceasing sexual activity after the menopause. Their spouse's reduced potency becomes a relief.

Other women were brought up to believe that sexual relations end at a certain age and that sexual fulfillment has a definite expiration date.

When Desire Seems Elusive

Although it's true that the most important sex organ in the human body is the brain, not all female sexual problems are mental. It's no surprise that desire can evaporate if sexual encounters lead to discomfort. When 52-year-old Alice started feeling chafed and experienced vaginal soreness for days after intercourse, her instinct was to avoid sex altogether. She thought there was something wrong with her body—she couldn't get the tiniest bit lubricated even if her mind was more than willing. Only when a friend mentioned that she was having similar problems did she realize that this was a natural change-of-life issue—one that could be easily solved.

Atrophic vaginitis is a condition that occurs in perimenopausal and menopausal women when the tissues around the vulva and the lining of the vagina become thin and easily damaged. This is the most common sexual complaint of all menopausal women and fortunately one that can be easily treated. Discussing the situation with your partner is important. Reassure him that it's not his fault, nor yours, just a natural part of the menopausal shift in hormones. Once he is aware, he can be more sensitive to your needs and not feel guilty or blame himself. That information alone can be a stress reducer and love enhancer. You might want to ask your partner if he has noticed any changes in your secretions. It's possible he might have felt too embarrassed to discuss it. By bringing your concerns up, it facilitates better communication about all sexual issues, including physical changes that he may be experiencing.

When estrogen levels become low, whether it is at menopause or after delivering a baby, all women will experience vaginal dryness and discomfort during intercourse unless they replenish the estrogen or use a natural and safe form of vaginal lubrication. Typically, small amounts of estrogen taken by vaginal cream or estradiol-containing vaginal rings are options for women who do not wish to use systemic hormones, or who need to supplement the hormone regime that they are already on. Alternatively, non–hormonally-based lubricants such as Astroglide, Replens, K-Y jelly, Maxilube, or even saliva can help. All of these therapies will help alleviate the physical discomfort. However, lack of desire can be due to the loss of testosterone, which has a profound effect upon libido and sexual desire in women as well as men.

Testosterone: Not for Men Only

Our ovaries do a fabulous job of manufacturing all the essential ingredients necessary to keep us feminine, fertile, womanly, and sexy. However, hormonal production drops dramatically during the perimenopausal and menopausal years and even more precipitously following a hysterectomy. Estrogen is not the only ovarian hormone to fall off the cliff. Testosterone, commonly thought of as a male hormone, is also produced in women and declines significantly after menopause. In particular, women who have had their ovaries surgically removed will experience an even more drastic change in hormone levels since the body does not have time to adapt to a gradual decline. It is not uncommon for a hysterectomized woman to suffer a loss of libido, even if she is on estrogen replacement. A little bit of testosterone can go a long way in restoring libido, energy, and even mental well-being. Testosterone is in fact the key hormonal ingredient driving libido. Of course, a couple's problems and each partner's personal problems can interfere with sexual function even when testosterone is normal.

Scientific studies conducted in the mid- and late 1990s showed that for menopausal women, testosterone supplementation improved sexual activity, sexual satisfaction, pleasure, and orgasm when compared to estrogen treatment alone. For women who had previously been receiving estrogen therapy, the addition of methyltestosterone (a modified form of testosterone) improved sexual desire and sensation over estrogen therapy alone.

Of all the proposed benefits of testosterone supplements for women, the advent of enhanced sexuality tops the list. Sexual desire, arousal, and increased frequency of sexual fantasies are positive effects of "vitamin T." In addition, depression is lessened, while cognitive function and memory are improved. And if that's not enough, the big T also improves muscle mass and bone stability and has a positive impact on metabolism. No wonder that with all these attributes of testosterone, women also experience improved mood and better energy summed up as a return of *joie de vivre*. Why wouldn't a woman want a little T? But a word of caution here. Too much of a good thing may not be good at all. Testosterone overdose can lead to oily skin, increased facial hair, male pattern baldness, and possible liver damage. Careful monitoring is necessary.

Don't Keep Me from My Testosterone!

Fifty-six-year-old Margie was a relatively new patient. She had been to several doctors in the few years since menopause, but felt she wasn't getting the type of care she was looking for. Although she was taking estrogen for menopausal hot flashes, she knew something was missing from her hormonal formula and was determined to find it. When a friend suggested she come speak to me, Margie was at a low point in her life. After a thorough history and a physical exam, Margie was surprised that I brought up the topic of sex. Not a single physician had asked her about her sex life before. And to make matters worse, Margie felt embarrassed to bring it up since she thought she was past the point in her life where sex was supposed to be important. When I assured her that as long as she was alive, she was still entitled to have sexual feelings, she burst into tears. That element of her life had vanished and she was overjoyed to hear that it could be restored. I asked her if she would be willing to try a little bit of testosterone. "Isn't that for men?" she asked sheepishly. I promised her that in small doses testosterone could be just as important for women and it wouldn't cause a beard to grow or her voice to deepen. Margie was more than willing to try.

After Margie's second month of low-dose testosterone injections, she felt like her old vital, robust self. Her energy levels zoomed, her libido came back, and her spirit and confidence levels were restored—so much so that when we called to cancel her appointment because of a power outage in the building, she insisted on coming in, climbing up several flights of stairs (she brought her flashlight), and getting her monthly dose of testosterone. "Nothing comes between me and my testosterone," she announced with a big grin. Testosterone supplements are also available in topical gels, creams, and, in the future, a patch for women.

Besides estrogen, it appears that testosterone may be a midlife woman's best friend. As the word gets out, more and more menopausal women will be asking for their daily dose of testosterone— and for good reason.

Other Sex Drain Culprits

For some perimenopausal women, low-dose birth control pills are recommended to control irregular bleeding and provide hormone balance during the transition. This can be quite helpful as well as practical in offering protection from a potential surprise pregnancy. The two populations of women who have the highest incidence of abortion for unplanned pregnancy include teenagers and perimenopausal women. And while the low-dose pill also offers the advantage of reducing the risk of ovarian cancer, for some women the birth control pill can diminish sexual desire. The pill increases the amount of sex hormone–binding globulin that circulates in the bloodstream. This in turn binds the free testosterone, making it unavailable to do the things that testosterone normally does to maintain libido. So one has to balance the positives with the potential negative side effects. The same can be said of antidepressants such as Prozac,

Zoloft, Elavil, Anafranil, and antianxiety agents such as Valium, Xanax, and Ativan, which may diminish arousal and cause orgasmic dysfunction.

Certainly health concerns of both partners can interfere with sexual enjoyment. If a man or a woman suffers from heart disease, it's not unusual for the spouse to worry about the effects of sexual exertion or even sexual excitement in precipitating a heart attack. Incontinence can also lead to embarrassment and sexual avoidance. Addressing these health concerns and understanding the real rather than the imagined impact upon sexual function can go a long way in improving relations for both men and women.

Sex and the Psyche

Many studies have shown a rise in depression and anxiety as we age. There is no question that this in turn has a direct effect on libido and the sexual response. A depressed woman will experience a loss of desire, and this in turn can cause a woman's sexual partner to stop initiating sexual relations. Chronic irritability may also be a sign of depression or could reflect marital discord. Both situations will lead to reduced libido for both partners. Altered body image such that a woman is ashamed or uncomfortable with the age-induced physical changes in her appearance can also obliterate sexual responsiveness and desire. Even if her partner still loves and appreciates her physical attributes, a woman may be so negative about her self image that she withdraws physically and sexually.

Happy Anniversary—Don't Touch Me!

Married for 24 years, Maureen and Herb love each other dearly in the traditional sense of caring for each other. However, their physical love had seemed to expire. When Maureen and Herb celebrated their twenty-fourth anniversary with a romantic candlelit dinner, Maureen felt she was somewhere else. Even the candles couldn't spark a sexy encounter that evening. Herb knew something was wrong but found it too hard to talk about.

When Herb celebrated his fifty-third birthday, he described his goals as "looking forward to enjoying the rest of my life." He felt fit and healthy.

Maureen, on the other hand, felt as if she were carrying a 500-pound gorilla on her back. Her energy levels were zippo. Her internist checked her out completely and told her all of her blood work was fine, including thyroid levels. She was started on a low-dose hormone supplement, but even that didn't seem to improve her mood or libido. "Mom, you're not yourself. I think you need to do something about this," urged her 22-year-old daughter, so Maureen went to a counselor. After two sessions, it became apparent that Maureen's joy of living had been sinking for the past one and a half years. It was important that she had had a full physical exam and was checked for such diseases as hypothryoidism. The hormone supplement seemed to help a bit, but there was still something missing. Mild to moderate depression was the diagnosis. A very low-dose antidepressant was prescribed and an aerobic exercise program was recommended.

After six months of treatment and feeling remarkably improved, Maureen was gradually weaned from the antidepressant medication but maintained her five-day-a-week aerobic walking program. Her energy levels and libido came back and have stayed there. She states she had been in the dark that she could have been depressed. She thought depression meant crying all the time. She didn't cry, but looking back she could tell that she had withdrawn, not only from herself but from her loving husband. She was happy that aerobic exercise could help maintain her better mood as well as improved energy levels. Bob felt he regained his wife's full loving nature.

A libido problem can sometimes be a complex issue. Almost always there can be help. Understanding the dynamics from the physical, physiological, hormonal, psychological, and relationship viewpoints gives the best perspective. Sometimes the solution can be remarkably simple.

Heartfelt Is More Romantic Than "Cardiacfelt"

When 63-year-old Frank suffered a mild heart attack, his doctor told him he was a lucky man: the mild event had led doctors to treat him so that he wouldn't have a recurrent and more major event. By having two stents placed in arteries that were nearly completely blocked, Frank was literally given a new lease on life. "Thank goodness for modern technology," Frank commented. "It's great to have a new plumbing system." He felt vigorous and happy that he no longer had that nagging but subtle chest pain. He had never talked about his chest pains in the past because he knew it would worry his 58-year-old wife Sylvia. Now that he was new and improved, he felt more comfortable initiating sex.

To his surprise, Sylvia was now the one reluctant to participate in foreplay—she even wanted to avoid sex altogether. Secretly fearing Frank still had a bad cardiac condition, she shot down his romantic overtures. All she could think of was Frank being monitored in the cardiac intensive care unit and it frightened the sexual feelings right out of her. Only when she accompanied Frank on a follow-up visit to his cardiologist's office did she get the reassurance she needed. For now, the cardiologist assured her, Frank was "good to go." He also asked Frank to promise that if he had recurrence of chest pain he would be honest and open about it. That way he could get early treatment if needed and Sylvia wouldn't have to hold back, worrying that he was still secretly experiencing chest pains. As the doctor explained, "Romance from the heart is definitely not a cardiac condition."

What's Age Got to Do with It?

Sometimes a woman may feel there is a certain age when it's not okay to be sexy. Whether this is a preprogrammed message or a cultural response is often difficult to distinguish. Sometimes we may think of our own mothers and/or grandmothers and have images that would not seem to be compatible with sexuality. Alternatively, some women may feel that this is the time of life when it is okay not to want to be sexy and seek relief from sexual activity, especially if sex was not enjoyable in the past. Menopause thus becomes a safe haven from undesired sexual activity. In reality, age has less to do with sexuality than the combined elements of overall physical health, mental acuity, hormonal intactness, and the overall desire to maintain sexual function. Having a willing, available, caring, and loving partner completes the formula.

Biological problems account for the majority of sexual problems in the menopausal age group. However, these problems rarely exist in the absence of psychological, sociocultural, and/or relationship issues. Therefore, a thorough evaluation should address these other, nonphysiological factors as well.

From a purely biological perspective, declining estrogen levels account for most sexual problems in menopause. This results in a condition known as hypoestrogenization of the pelvic tissues. Loss of clitoral sensation in close to 20 percent of menopause-aged women is the result of less stimulation by the pudendal nerve. This in turn causes a delay in reaching orgasm or even the complete absence of orgasm. Vaginal dryness is also an important issue affecting 31 percent of menopausal women. Vaginismus is a consequence of vaginal dryness because the woman develops a conditioned reflex to painful sex—the muscles of the vagina contract such that the male penis cannot penetrate. Dyspareunia, or painful intercourse, resulting from vaginal dryness is relatively easy to treat and should be taken care of before vaginismus develops. If a woman has vaginismus, it is much more difficult to correct and often a sex therapist must be consulted.

Loss of sexual desire affects close to 40 percent of perimenopausal and menopausal women. This can be the result of multi-hormonal problems involving estrogen as well as androgen. The combination of estrogen deficiency leading to vaginal atrophy and reduced clitoral sensitivity, and androgen deficiency leading to loss of libido, can obliterate sexual satisfaction.

Besides hormonal issues, marital problems are one of the most common reasons for a decline in sexual activity. And it does make a difference if the marital problems are new or long-standing. Acute marital problems may be a consequence of less sex secondary to hormonal issues. When libido issues are treated medically, marital problems tend to resolve. Chronic marital problems tend to be more complex and difficult to treat but should be evaluated from the emotional, physical, and hormonal perspectives as well. Women whose marriages have been on a steady downturn may have built up tremendous resentment toward their spouse and may look forward to menopause to justify terminating sexual relations. There may also be a cultural bias that suggests menopause is a time of asexuality.

Communicating about Sex

Over 55 percent of women indicate that their health care provider never initiates discussions about sexual function. Only 3 percent report that discussion is initiated at every office visit. Many women don't feel comfortable bringing up the topic if it apparently wasn't deemed appropriate by their physician. Women may feel they may be put down for initiating a discussion and are therefore reluctant to admit that they are suffering from sexual difficulties. Yet studies have shown that within two years of the start of menopause, there is typically a 50 percent decline in sexual desire, a 50 percent decrease in coital frequency, and a 50 percent decline in orgasm. With the aging of the baby boomer population, sexual problems are entering the realm of a major public health problem of epidemic proportions. It behooves the medical profession to become more proactive in addressing these conditions.

Even if her health care provider doesn't bring up the topic, a woman should feel an obligation to herself not to let this important area of concern slide if she or her partner is concerned. Discussing and clarifying the problem can prove to be very helpful, and health care providers today are improving in this capacity. If there is not enough time at your office visit, make a follow-up appointment. If your physician is not comfortable or is inexperienced in discussing sexual issues, ask for a referral to someone who is.

CHAPTER 5

Midlife Sexuality: The Male Perspective

His Penis Saved His Life . . . and Other Stories

Harry has always led a very full life. At the age of 49, he was promoted to CEO of his rapidly expanding Internet startup and was spending more time traveling than on the home front. Although he complained about the time away from his wife and three children, he secretly relished the excitement of it all. The only problem was the toll his lifestyle seemed to be having on his sex life. While all the travel was admittedly fatiguing, his libido was not affected in the least. But why wouldn't his penis cooperate? Even though he desperately wanted to have sexual relations with his wife, he just couldn't sustain an erection. Embarrassed by the apparent lack of function, he hid the problem from his wife and just kept telling her he was "too jet-lagged out" to think about sex.

Harry's wife, Debbie, an attractive 45-year-old blonde who prided herself in keeping in top shape, was beginning to wonder. After a three-week reprieve from the travel circuit, Harry was still complaining of jet lag. Was Harry being unfaithful while he was on the road? Was she losing her appeal? After months of wondering and worrying and bouts of self-doubt, she confronted Harry. Finally Debbie gathered all her courage, preparing herself for what she thought would be the question that ended their 25-year marriage: "Harry, you have to tell me the truth. Who are you having an affair with?"

Harry turned pale as all the pent-up emotions drained from his body. "What on earth makes you think that?" he demanded to know.

"Well, it's obvious you have no interest in me," Debbie grunted back at him.

This was the moment Harry needed. Keeping his dark secret was no longer working for him and certainly wasn't nurturing the relationship with the only woman he cared about, his wife Debbie. He could hardly contain himself as he told her about his months of self-doubt and denial.

Once Debbie learned the truth, she was relieved about their relationship, but at the same time worried about Harry's health. She emphatically insisted that Harry go for a long-overdue physical. And it was just in the nick of time. Although Harry didn't have any other signs or symptoms, his tests revealed severe atherosclerosis (hardening of the arteries) and this was the reason why he wasn't having normal erections.

The official term was *erectile dysfunction,* or ED. His doctor also told him he was lucky he hadn't succumbed to a sudden heart attack. He was scheduled the next day for angioplasty, a procedure to clean out the plaque from his coronary arteries. He also committed himself to a healthier lifestyle with regular exercise, lower-fat foods, and less travel. The results were worth it. Harry now has a healthier body, a happier marriage, and a rekindled sex life. In a sense, losing his denial about erectile dysfunction helped Harry regain his life.

Physical Causes of Erectile Dysfunction

Erectile dysfunction, or ED, the inability to attain and maintain an erection sufficient for vaginal penetration and satisfactory sexual performance, is a very common problem, affecting between 20 million and 30 million men in the United States. If we count the partners of these men, then it can be estimated that at least 40 million to 60 million Americans are in some way affected by ED. Clever marketers of herbal supplements geared for a midlife male audience have headlines shouting: "Your Sex Organ Is Shrinking"—a statement that is almost guaranteed to catch an innocent man's attention.

The good news is that most cases of erectile dysfunction are easily treated. The bad news is that too many men deny that they have a problem and look for excuses for either avoiding sex or reasons to blame their partner. This can have a domino effect causing the partner to either feel guilty, resentful, or suspicious of an affair, and the relationship falls apart. The woman may start to blame herself for not being attractive enough. The man may project his disappointment with himself onto his mate. The original problem doesn't go away but the denial might persist to the point where the man tries to prove his capability by bedding a new partner.

In the landmark Massachusetts Male Aging Study examining male sexuality, comprehensive medical, psychological, and hormonal evaluations were performed on over 1,700 men between the ages of 40 and 70. The results were published in the January 1994 issue of *The Journal of Urology* and the research is ongoing. The findings were surprising to say the least. More than 50 percent of all American men over age 40 had experienced some form of erectile dysfunction.

There was a consistent age-related decline in frequency of erections, difficulty in achieving and maintaining erections, and decreased incidence of erections upon awakening. As age increased, ejaculation problems also increased while sexual desire diminished. This translates into roughly twice the previous estimates of male sexual dysfunction and suggests that approximately 20 million men nationally suffer from some type of erection problem. How each man might react to sexual dysfunction is difficult to determine. However, the scientific community is able to discuss what the key causes of the dysfunction are and ultimately recommend solutions.

As recently as the 1970s and 1980s, it was believed that over 80 percent of poor erectile function was the result of psychological causes. However, more recent research reveals that physiological and physical factors are more significant. Perhaps these findings will help remove the stigma associated with erectile or sexual problems and free men to seek help and improve the quality of their lives—and their relationships.

The physical causes of erectile dysfunction include all medical conditions that result in diminished blood flow to the penis. Medical problems that have a vascular component such as diabetes, hypertension, and atherosclerosis are all culprits. Even a nonmedical situation such as too much pressure to the pelvic region during prolonged bicycle riding could cause numbing of the genital region and secondary erectile dysfunction.

Erections occur when there is a net increase in blood flow to the penis causing engorgement strong enough for intercourse. If there is a deficiency in the amount of blood flow, a full erection cannot be maintained, no matter the degree of excitation. Many men are often surprised to discover that high blood sugar (diabetes) can cause problems with potency. Similarly, atherosclerosis, which causes high blood pressure, can also result in diminished erections.

Ironically, some of the medications used to treat these conditions can also have the side effect of erectile dysfunction. Losing erectile efficiency may be a very potent warning sign for men to have a comprehensive health evaluation to discover the underlying cause. Atherosclerosis can be an invisible but deadly disease until it gives us some warning. Perhaps ED is Mother Nature's way of getting a man's attention that all is not well beneath the surface. Excessive alcohol, smoking, and drug abuse are also common causes of diminished sexual function.

Psychological Causes of Erectile Dysfunction

Which came first, the chicken or the egg? "Mr. Smith, were you depressed before or after you lost your erections?" Sometimes the condition may seem obvious but the answer is not apparent. Both anxiety and depression reduce a man's libido and interfere with the thought processes necessary for arousal. Ironically, some of the medications used to treat depression and anxiety have side effects of reduced libido and impotence. That is why it is important to have a thorough evaluation, which includes a comprehensive history and physical exam, before starting treatment.

Prozac, Paxil, Zoloft, and Effexor are antidepressants with the known side effects of abnormal ejaculation, decreased libido, and impotence. Unfortunately there is no single ideal pharmacological agent for the treatment of male midlife depression that is free of potential side effects. The benefits of regular exercise, including walking, can lead to enhanced levels of circulating beta-endorphins (a natural mood elevator released into the bloodstream) and act as a natural antidepressant.

Sometimes the cause for erectile dysfunction might be multifactorial. Men who suffer from clinical depression are more than twice as likely to develop coronary artery disease in comparison to nondepressed men. Now that's a fact to be doubly depressed about! The study was supported by the National Institute of Aging and conducted at Johns Hopkins University. Daniel Ford, M.D., M.P.H., lead author, concluded: "Clinical depression appears to be an independent risk factor for coronary artery disease, even several decades after the first episode." The message to clinicians treating men with depression or heart disease is to look for the existence of an accompanying disorder and to consider the potential impact on sexual function as well.

Changes in Sexual Behavior in the MidLife Male

Perhaps the change in sexual functioning can be considered man's greatest fear of facing midlife. Too often couples fall prey to the belief of expecting consistency in their sexual relationship and are then often misled by unrealistic images of movie romance and sexuality. What is normal in the younger male is no longer standard for an older man—and both men and women need to be aware of these differences. For example, a young male may achieve an erection in seconds while a man in his 50s and 60s may require several minutes for the same response. Ejaculations are typically less full and less forceful, and the refractory period, on time to recover, may extend to days rather than minutes. This is typical and normal despite what the silver screen would have us believe.

But now there's a little blue pill with the promise of better erections through chemistry: Viagra. Is this truly God's gift to man or a way of the denial of aging in midlife men? For some men, it's a dream come true; for some women, a nightmare. For the medical community, Viagra marks a dramatic change in awareness about a previously well-kept secret: male impotence.

A positive side effect of Viagra has been the scheduling of long-overdue medical checkups for men who haven't been to a physician in years. It's an opportunity to practice good preventive medicine in a population that traditionally might avoid seeing a doctor altogether. The physician should recommend checking cholesterol levels, as well as performing prostate cancer screening, performing a thorough physical exam, monitoring PSA levels (prostate-specific antigen) as well as discussing weight and lifestyle issues. Perhaps for this reason alone, Viagra can be considered a step forward for men's health.

However, Viagra, or sildenafil citrate, is certainly not a panacea for all things sexual in men or women. If a man has diminished libido or a complete loss of sexual desire, Viagra will not offer much relief. The chemical formula of Viagra works to relax the smooth muscles in the blood vessels and allow for greater blood flow to the penis. It serves to pump up erections where there is a blood flow problem. It is analogous to a penis enhancer. It does not have a stimulatory effect on the brain to enhance or create sexual excitement, nor does it enhance a woman's mood or offer romantic overtures.

For some women, the advent of Viagra for men has been seen as another blow to female sexuality. As my sweet 70-year-old patient, Rosie, confided, "Ever since Charlie has gotten that Viagra stuff, he feels he needs to show it off. Without the appetizers, I don't care for the main course anymore!" Perhaps physicians who prescribe Viagra for their elderly male patients should include a refresher course on romance, fondling, patience, kindness, and good old-fashioned sweet talk. More women would respond to those attributes than the resurrection of the old stiff rod.

Sexual Desire versus Sexual Function

"Which came first, the loss of your sexual desire or the loss of your erections?" was the question put as gently as nails scratching a chalkboard to 58-year-old George. Here he was in his own doctor's office and he was wishing he had been told he had just one more second to live so he could escape with a good excuse. "Doc, I just don't know." Thank goodness the office door was shut. George was relieved to hear that the questioning was over—for now. "We'll run some blood tests and see about your testosterone levels," his doctor said. A nurse came in to draw his blood—George was grateful that this was a less painful experience than the interview. Two weeks later George learned that his testosterone level was low and his libido could be improved with some supplementation. He was mightily relieved to know that there was a remedy for his problem.

Sometimes it is difficult to distinguish the primary cause of sexual dysfunction. It helps to have a sympathetic, experienced, and tactful physician to turn to. Fortunately, more physicians are becoming better versed in problems of sexuality and there is greater expertise available to patients. Sometimes men with erectile failure develop low sexual desire as a result of the embarrassment of not being able to sustain an erection. However, the reverse may also be true. A man may be physically capable of having a normal erection, but if the desire is not there he is less likely to achieve one. Treatment strategies will depend upon an accurate assessment of the hormonal and physical status of the man as well as the health of the relationship.

In George's case, a testosterone deficiency was discovered. The drop in his testosterone levels contributed to his loss of desire, which in turn prevented him from having a normal erection. In a short amount of time he was so worried about what was happening to the symbol of his masculinity—his erectile function—that he forgot about the desire problem. Fortunately, his libido returned with a small amount of testosterone. Not only did his erections come back, but he felt like he had renewed energy—and hope.

How Do I Know If I Am Testosterone Deficient?

Testosterone supplementation can be a man's best friend if there is a true deficiency. Otherwise, too much of a good thing can be harmful. To determine if you are truly testosterone deficient, your physician will want to do a full physical exam and measure levels of total testosterone, free testosterone, as well as sex hormone–binding globulin. For older men, the issue of the diagnosis of testosterone deficiency is not always clear-cut. All men experience a continuous and slow decline in serum testosterone levels after about age thirty, with an average drop of 1 to 2 percent a year. Obesity, smoking, hypothyroidism, certain medications, and severe systemic diseases can all accelerate the loss of testosterone.

The actual decline in testosterone production with age is the result of a decrease in the manufacture of this steroid hormone by the testes themselves. There is a loss in the number of Leydig cells—the little factories that manufacture this potent product. In addition, there is a blunting of the response to higher hormonal signals coming from the brain pleading for more testosterone to be pumped into the bloodstream.

These pituitary hormonal messengers include follicle-stimulating hormone (FSH) as well as luteinizing hormone (LH), and are referred to as gonadotropin-stimulating hormones. They in turn are under the command of the hypothalamus, an even higher brain command center. The gonadotropin stimulating-releasing hormones rise in the older male as the levels of the end product—testosterone—wane.

This biological supply-and-demand network forms the basis of the body's finely tuned endocrine feedback loop. It is a brilliant system and physicians capitalize on this knowledge. It is standard therapy to measure blood FSH and LH levels in perimenopausal and menopausal women to assess the need for hormone replacement. In women, these hormone levels rise even more robustly as an indication of declining estrogen production. In men, FSH and LH levels are measured as a supplement to testosterone measurements.

Finally, serum levels of sex hormone–binding globulin (SHBG) must be taken into account to get an accurate assessment of real-time testosterone availability. Because serum levels of SHBG increase with age, the decline in levels of free, or bioavailable, testosterone is often much greater than the decline in total testosterone and may give an inaccurate picture of true hormonal responsiveness. That is why it is absolutely critical not to rely on a single blood sample measuring total testosterone levels. It may not reflect the actual amount of unbound testosterone that is available to work on the receptors and do the job. It is very possible that a man's total testosterone is normal but his levels of bioavailable testosterone are deficient. If non-SHBG-bound testosterone is used as the determining measurement, as many as 50 percent of men age 60 or more could be testosterone deficient.

Timing may be a critical factor in measuring your body's testosterone production as well. A morning sample is recommended because of the known circadian rhythm in testosterone release in men younger than 60 years of age. Testosterone levels are highest in the early morning hours and can drop by 35 percent in the afternoon and evening hours. Since testosterone is secreted in a pulsatile (discrete pulses at regular intervals) fashion, two samples taken slightly apart may give a more reliable measurement. After age 60 the circadian nature of testosterone production becomes blunted and it is probably not as critical to get an early-morning reading.

If the total plasma testosterone level is less than 7.0 nm/L (200 ng/dL), this is a very clear indication of hypogonadism regardless of age, and further evaluation is necessary. Thyroid disorders as well as pituitary tumors must be ruled out by measuring prolactin hormone and thyroid hormone levels. MRI studies of the pituitary gland may be necessary to rule out the presence of a pituitary tumor, especially if prolactin levels are abnormally high.

When the lower level of normal for total testosterone is used to define testosterone deficiency, approximately 11 to 36 percent of older men will fall into this category. However, when the more precise measurement of non-SHBG-bound testosterone is used as the defining criterion, as many as 50 percent of men age 60 and above would be considered testosterone deficient and possible candidates for supplementation.

What to Expect after Starting Testosterone Therapy

Before starting on testosterone supplementation, it is crucial to check that the prostate is normal and there is no occult or hidden prostate cancer. Just as a woman should have a mammogram before starting on estrogen replacement therapy to rule out breast cancer, a man needs to be sure that he is free of prostate cancer.

If you start testosterone, what type of benefits can you expect? To begin with, many men immediately feel an improvement in their libido. This is accompanied by enhanced mood and overall psychological well-being. Some studies have also indicated an improvement in cognitive function, as well as enhanced strength and stamina. Other goals may be to prevent osteoporosis by preserving bone mass and to improve lean body mass and overall function.

Over seven studies have shown an increase in bone density and a slowing of bone degradation in men on testosterone therapy. The benefits in enhancing bone mineral density in men on testosterone therapy have been of similar magnitude to those in postmenopausal women given estrogen replacement.

Some studies suggest that androgen therapy in men may decrease cardiovascular risk. Most epidemiological evidence supports a correlation between higher total serum testosterone levels and lower cardiovascular disease. The type of androgens used for hormone replacement therapy in older men—that is, the circulating androgens such as testosterone—actually can lower total cholesterol and LDL cholesterol serum levels while having little impact on serum HDL cholesterol levels. In addition, testosterone may act as a vasodilator, allowing better blood flow to the heart. Some studies have even shown that androgen administration can reduce visceral fat accumulation which is linked to increased cardiovascular risk. Less fat, less risk.

Although certainly not a panacea for all things male and aging, testosterone definitely offers a variety of intriguing benefits. In general, men with low libido have gained the most benefits in having their sex drives revamped. Although erectile dysfunction in men over age 50 is rarely caused by androgen deficiency, this condition may occasionally improve with testosterone therapy.

Aside from libido issues, testosterone has a positive effect on mood and overall psychological well-being. It might function as a mild antidepressive for midlife men with low moods and low blood testosterone levels. One distinct benefit of testosterone over other antidepressants is that it doesn't cause ejaculatory or impotency problems as a side effect. Although becoming the ultimate macho male is not a realistic indication for starting testosterone replacement, there is no question that a man's strength, stamina, muscle mass, and bone density can improve. This in turn can prevent falls and lessen the possibility of life-threatening hip fractures.

Contraindications and Possible Risks of Testosterone Therapy

An absolute contraindication is the presence of prostate or breast cancer. Every midlife male, whether or not he is considering testosterone therapy, must be screened for prostate cancer by having a physical exam of the prostate and measurement of blood prostate-specific antigen (PSA) levels. If the prostate is abnormally large or if the PSA level is elevated, a man should be referred for ultrasound and biopsy of the prostate before starting any androgen therapy. Androgens have a potential role in promoting both benign prostatic hyperplasia (BPH), or tissue overgrowth, and prostate cancer. With approximately over 180,000 newly diagnosed cases of prostatic cancer each year, over 37,000 men die annually from this disease. Hidden prostate cancers are detectable in 25 percent of men under age 40 and the overall incidence is approximately 50 percent higher in African Americans. Fortunately, most studies in older men have reported no significant change in PSA or other prostate parameters with testosterone replacement.

Since testosterone is metabolized in the male body to estrogen, too much testosterone could result in breast enlargement, or gynecomastia—not an attractive side effect for most macho males. If a man suffers from sleep apnea, it is possible that this condition could worsen in the presence of too much male hormone. Sleep apnea is prevalent in middle-aged and older men, and screening is recommended. In addition, fluid retention and possibly increased risk for heart disease could be the consequence of an overabundance of testosterone. However, no studies of testosterone replacement in older men have revealed worsening of hypertension, congestive heart failure, or peripheral edema.

What Types of Testosterone Therapy Are Available?

If you decide to take testosterone, what is the best formulation for you? Ideally, taking testosterone as a supplement should be safe, convenient, inexpensive, and produce physiological levels to correct the clinical deficiency. By creating as natural a blood level as possible, the goal is to avoid potential short-term as well as long-term side effects. Testosterone is available in oral, injectable, transdermal, and implantable formulations.

The oral forms of testosterone include fluoxymesterone, methyltestosterone, and oxandrolone, and are not recommended for androgen replacement therapy because of the potential for serious liver damage. They also may raise serum LDL cholesterol levels, decrease HDL cholesterol levels, and have been implicated in premature heart attack and stroke.

Intramuscular injections have been the mainstay of testosterone therapy for many years and have been supported by the greatest amount of clinical data on their safety and efficacy. Usually, the dosage is 400 mg every two to four weeks. While this method is effective and inexpensive, in some men there can be wide variations in serum testosterone levels leading to fluctuations in mood, energy level, libido, and sexual function.

More recently, the Food and Drug Administration has approved scrotal and nonscrotal transdermal patches for androgen replacement therapy. These systems provide for more natural levels of testosterone imitating the circadian rhythm of higher levels in the morning and lower levels in the evening. Unfortunately, this method is sometimes associated with skin irritation at the application site—up to 10 percent of patients enrolled in clinical trials and 30 to 50 percent of men in clinical practice discontinued the patch because of this side effect.

Testosterone has also been fused into pellets that can be implanted beneath the skin. Advantages of this technique are that it is convenient and normal-range serum testosterone levels can be achieved for up to six months. The downside is that a minor surgical procedure is initially needed for implantation. However, this modality has many advocates and should soon become available in the United States.

What If I Decide to Start Testosterone Therapy?

Typically it is recommended that therapy be continued for at least six months to one year, with a follow-up appointment within the first three months to check for any adverse effects. A serum testosterone level should also be checked to see if there is a need for dosage adjustment. Your doctor should also evaluate your blood pressure, blood count (hemoglobin/hematocrit), and PSA levels to confirm that they are in the normal range. As with any medical treatment, the risk-benefit ratio of testosterone replacement therapy must be carefully considered and continually evaluated.

Other Factors Affecting Midlife Male Sexuality

Therapists often suggest to their patients that the penis is attached to the heart. What this implies is that a man's feelings are central to his sexual capabilities. This core concept becomes more important as a man grows older. The influence of life circumstances, his relationship and feelings for his partner, his perception of himself as a lover, as well as his own sense of masculinity play a more significant role in a man's sexual performance as he ages. Mood plays a role in sexual function as well, while emotional and physical stress also add to the hormonal milieu.

Midlife represents the crossroads of psychological vulnerability and hormonal instability. In a manner reminiscent of adolescence, there is a constant interplay between hormones, mood, and life events. While a midlife man can't help but notice changes on the outside, the internal transition may represent the greatest challenge for himself and his partner.

CHAPTER 6

Understanding and Embracing
This Important Time

I must confess I stand to be corrected. For most of my adult life I have been operating under the premise that a crisis implies a negative and/or life-threatening event. Even as a physician, working under stressful circumstances in the emergency room, we frequently referred to life or death situations as crisis events. The media has helped promote the public perception that a crisis has only a negative connotation, as in the Middle East crisis, the energy crisis, the hostage crisis, or the crisis in the White House. Let those of us who are under a similar misperception of the true meaning of crisis stand to be corrected.

According to *Webster's New World Dictionary*, a crisis is defined as (1) the turning point of a disease for better or worse; (2) a decisive or crucial time, stage, or event. Being a natural-born skeptic, I felt compelled to get a second opinion, and sure enough *The American Heritage Dictionary* concurs. So I propose that we officially embrace midlife crisis as a turning point in adult life that brings potential for improvement. Perhaps it is time to update our concept of midlife crisis.

Midlife: A New Perspective on the Crisis Situation

Just as puberty doesn't occur overnight, nor does midlife transition for either man or woman. As every parent of a teenager knows, adolescence has its ups and downs. Officially defined as the physical and psychological development that occurs between childhood and adulthood, adolescence and puberty are highlighted by marked hormonal shifts. Parents often brace themselves for this landmark rite of passage. And just as puberty has been acknowledged multiculturally as an evolution in the physical being and emotional self, so, too, should midlife transition.

If the psychological mind-set of puberty is immortality caught in a sea of raging hormones, then the analogous mind-set of midlife is down-to-earth mortality faced in a changing hormonal and physical vessel. In both scenarios, fluctuating hormones may contribute to individuals acting out of character. It is understandable that hormonal fluctuations in both men and women have an impact on our behavior, mood, sexuality, cognitive function, outlook on life, and overall function. While there are no precise road maps for either journey, there are guideposts and some guidelines to help us along the way.

Opportunity or Dilemma?

"We share each other's adventures at the end of the day," is the way 65-year-old Georgette describes her evenings with her retired 68-year-old physician husband, Larry. However, Georgette and Larry are not rocking in front of the fireplace and reminiscing about the day's golf game or events at the bridge club. The couple in this mature and loving 45-year-strong marriage are discussing the happenings at their respective postretirement volunteer positions. They are having the time of their life helping to improve the educational opportunities and medical facilities at a rural outpost in Nigeria. Not your typical retirement couple.

Larry is retired from a full-time faculty position at an acclaimed university medical center while Georgette holds a Ph.D. in education and taught undergraduates at a private liberal arts college. Georgette's title is officially that of "visiting lecturer" (they have been visiting for two years now), but she has unofficially been ushered in as dean at the Nigerian college where she teaches. She likes to remind Larry that *"dean* is a four-letter word" when she has to make decisions that cannot please all the faculty or students. Likewise, Larry has his challenges teaching medicine at a hospital where it is difficult, if not impossible, to get prescriptions filled or diagnostic procedures accomplished or even routine blood work screened.

What made them do this in lieu of a comfortable, cozy retirement back in Southern California? Larry quickly pipes up, "This was all Georgette's idea—I just came along for the ride." Clearly they are both on the same wavelength. While it is true that this was initially Georgette's brainchild, Larry was a willing partner in giving it a try. He knew that his wife had always encouraged her students to use their talents where they could make the most impact for the good of man—even if it meant going to a third-world nation. So here they were, thriving in the golden years of their life, helping others, living out a lifelong ambition, and making a difference in the world.

They admit that some of their friends thought they were a bit looney and were going through some sort of midlife crisis. However, Larry's respect for Georgette's vision and his own willingness to participate made this couple's midlife crisis a true opportunity. They have never felt happier or more satisfied with their lives. There was always the understanding that if the situation was not working well for both of them, they would not allow one partner to be in duress as the other blossomed.

While this particular situation is certainly not every midlife couple's cup of tea, the principles of having a vision for the future, sharing mutual respect and appreciation of each other, as well as showing a willingness to work together can maintain a strong partnership.

Anima and Animus

Marcy and Ken have been together for their entire adult life. Having met and fallen in love in high school, the couple married while both were in college, but it was Marcy who quit in her junior year to help support the growing family. As Marcy fondly recalls, "Ken swept me off my feet in high school, and I've been sweeping ever since." Ken graduated from college with honors and followed a successful career path while Marcy kept the ship afloat at home. Twenty years of marriage and four children later, Marcy was delighted that their youngest was soon to graduate from high school, move out of the house, and go off to college. Ken, in sharp contrast, felt reluctant to let their youngest go off and worried what the household would feel like as an empty nest.

Marcy gleefully admitted that she was finally coming into her own. As the kids grew up and started high school and college, Marcy began to reclaim her education and sanity. Taking courses part-time, she proved to be an outstanding student and would soon be graduating with a business degree and honors to boot. Most importantly, she felt energized and had a burning desire to start a new enterprise. For years she had suppressed, perhaps consciously as well as unconsciously, her dreams of accomplishment outside of the household. She felt her turn had come. After all, she had helped put Ken through school first and then all the kids.

Ken, on the other hand, was counting the days to a well-deserved retirement, enhancing his life with more leisure and more travel. One of his dreams was to take cooking lessons and become an at-home gourmet. He often joked about becoming the Martha Stewart of their neighborhood and looked forward to being surrounded by a stack of cookbooks in the kitchen. Ken was definitely changing course and revving down while Marcy was revving up. What was really going on? Was this a normal midlife transition, a role reversal, or some-thing else?

Jungian psychologists might look at the above scenario and ex-plain it in terms of *anima* and *animus*. Jung postulated that for each of us, whatever is true in our conscious attitude, there is an attitude representing the opposite view that resides in our unconscious. While the ego consciousness identifies with the biological sex, a complementary contrasexual personality exists within the uncon-scious core. The anima therefore represents a man's unconscious feminine side, while the animus is a woman's unconscious mascu-line side. Midlife appears to lower the threshold for the expression of anima and animus. During the menopausal transition, there is a rela-tive increase in the ratio of male-to-female hormones as estrogen lev-els diminish and androgens increase. Similarly in the andropausal male, androgen levels decline and the relative ratio of female hor-mone increases.

As men and women both experience changing hormonal thresh-old levels during middle age, it is not surprising that their physiology and psyches reflect these changes. For some individuals, there is a frightened denial that these changes are occurring in the mind and body. For others, this is a midlife awakening, a time to reevaluate life and reassess the direction of one's life and true dreams and goals. A midlife unsettling might occur. But an awareness and an appreciation and actual embracing of this hormonal and psychologi-cal shift is a healthy event. As Jung himself reflected on this time of life in *Boundaries of the Soul: The Practice of Jung's Psychology,* "We cannot live the afternoon of life according to the program of life's morning; for what was great in the morning will be little at evening, and what in the morning was true will at evening have be-come a lie."

For Ken and Marcy, the animus and anima were participating in their midlife evolution. Marcy was becoming free of her domestic re-sponsibilities. She described menopause as a launch pad for chal-lenging her ambitions and her animus in the more male-oriented business world. At the same time, Ken was becoming more in touch with his inner anima and was looking forward to living a less aggressive, cutthroat type of existence where his main function in life was warrior and breadwinner. Now he wanted to kick back, bake the bread, and smell the roses.

Neither Marcy nor Ken was going through a midlife crisis, although both would readily admit to being at a turning point in their lives. Fortunately, Ken was not threatened by Marcy's evolving sense of business power and took pride in her accomplishments. They were able to be flexible enough to accommodate each other's needs. Marcy made sure she wasn't turning into a workaholic and scheduled breaks and vacation time so she and Ken could relax together. Ken felt comfortable on the home scene and took pleasure in his new hobbies. What was unfolding simultaneously was their natural adaptation to their own biological, psychological, and physiological shifts. They were able to honor each other individually and emerge as a couple with a new script.

Have a Midlife Mission Statement

"Now that you are at this stage of life, what goals are you working toward?" I asked Tony, my patient's frustrated, 50-something husband. He had come along to the office visit at his wife's insistence, somewhat reluctantly, to understand her change of life. He had no clue that he, too, was embarking upon a midlife passage. He thought he was here just for Rhonda.

"We don't have to work at fifty, it just happens," was the curt response I received. Since I knew this man was a CEO of a moderate-sized corporation, I had to give him something he could immediately relate to. The first thing that popped into my mind was his corporate mission statement.

"Do you have a corporate mission statement?" I asked bluntly.

"Of course we do!" he retorted with a twinge of defensiveness in his tone.

"Well, if your corporation had a major shift, be it in personnel or long-term direction or philosophy, would it be worthwhile to reevaluate your mission statement?" I asked with a hint of a smile. I could tell he was beginning to get my drift. "You see," I continued, "you don't have to work to turn fifty, but you do have to work to keep the ship floating at fifty. Now that there has been a change in personnel (i.e., the kids have left home) and the corporate focus has changed (i.e., concentrating on running a busy full-time household and providing a college education for three children), what is the new mission statement?"

Rhonda perked up. "I would like our mission statement to be 'a mature but growing marriage based upon trust, unconditional love, and respect for each other.' "

"May I add something?" Tony whispered.

"Yes, of course, dear," Rhonda said, squeezing his hand.

Tony cleared his throat. "Our mission in marriage is to have trust, unconditional love and respect for each other, while enjoying each other for who we are."

I felt my mission with this couple was on the right track. After breaking through his own initial resistance, Tony was all ears in wanting to learn as much as possible about his wife's changes and his own changes at this time of life. Being an executive, Tony decided to make an executive decision and started a men's group at his company to address male midlife passage. Talk about having a turnaround student. Rhonda was as thrilled as a new bride taking off on a honeymoon to Hawaii. The new attitude had a wonderful effect on their love life as well.

Have you thought about your midlife mission statement? Even if you never had a marital mission statement before, now is a wonderful opportunity to create one together. Be playful. Think of your own mission statement separately and then together.

Here are some suggestions to get you started:

1. Begin with, "Our mission in marriage is to . . ."

2. Think about your true desires for each other.

3. What were some of your early dreams?

4. Now that you are in a new stage of life, what changes would you appreciate?

5. What are your goals for yourself and for each other?

6. Write a list of 10 wishes for yourself and then 10 wishes for your partner. Share them and compare what your desires are. You may have some items in common, such as "I want to travel to foreign countries," while others may not be related such as, "I want to breed fox terriers" or "I want to volunteer my time in a children's orphanage." The wish lists definitely need not overlap. Those areas that are identical might be incorporated into the mission statement as goals you desire to enjoy together. Other wishes that are distinct for each partner become fun topics to explore.

7. Perhaps you can help your partner achieve a longtime ambition to grow organic vegetables as a hobby or to take up art or photography or whatever. You each may become aware of desires or interests that previously were unknown. What a fun way to discover new things about your own partner and help or surprise him or her in fulfilling a dream! It may also give you insight as to his or her new ambitions.

8. Achieving a healthy balance of time together and time apart is also critical. The right blend of space and cohesiveness becomes a formula for success. Having too much togetherness may become tedious just as too much separateness may make us feel like strangers. Your mission statement may include general principles such as "Our goal is to spend quality time together" and then go on to be more specific: "Our desire is not to be apart for more than seven days in a row. We plan to share the same bedtime hour at least three quarters of the time."

Honor your mission statement. Give it value—make it permanent and have it printed. If you are artistic, perhaps you could print it in calligraphy or have a professional help you. Then display your mission statement where you can refer to it daily. Those who come into your home and see it may be inspired as well. It just might help their relationship, too.

Seven Essential Facts about His Andropause

1. Andropause is a real physiological event with true hormonal changes. Over 25 million men in the United States between the ages of 40 and 45 experience symptoms related to the male change of life.

2. Most men are not aware that they, too, like women, can experience hormonal changes that affect their sexual abilities, physical capabilities, and emotional stability. You may be more mindful of his change of life than he is. After all, you have had more preparation and experience with your own monthly changes.

3. Mood changes related to andropause include depression, irritability, anxiety, indecisiveness, and emotional changeability. A man may need more understanding and tender loving care during this time.

4. Physical changes related to andropause include loss of muscle mass, increased abdominal girth, fatigue, sleep disturbances, and hot flashes.

5. Sexual changes are common, with over 50 percent of men between the ages of 40 and 70 experiencing some degree of erectile failure. In general, erections are not as firm and take longer to achieve.

6. Many men are in denial that they might be experiencing some form of male menopause. The medical community is only just beginning to recognize the hormonal, physical, and emotional changes that men experience at this time of life.

7. Every midlife male should have a complete physical exam including prostate exam, blood PSA levels, and a hormonal evaluation. Men should be encouraged to discuss the symptoms they are experiencing and receive appropriate treatment. Offer to join your partner

for a couple's visit to the physician so you can learn more about his change of life.

Seven Essential Facts about Her Menopause

1. A woman does not go through menopause overnight. Typically, there is a perimenopausal transition that occurs from the mid- to late 40s. During this time, hormonal levels are changing and symptoms ranging from hot flashes and mood swings to sleep disturbances and irregular bleeding can occur to varying degrees. The average age for menopause is 51.5 years and by age 55 most women will have stopped having periods.

2. A woman may become more emotional during the menopausal transition and needs more understanding and tender loving care during this time.

3. Menopause is not the end of your sex life.

4. Lack of estrogen causes vaginal dryness and can make intercourse uncomfortable or painful. Fortunately, there are treatments available, both hormonal and nonhormonal, that effectively correct the problem. Be mindful of this potential problem and make sure there is adequate lubrication before having intercourse. Extra cuddling is always helpful.

5. She may feel more vulnerable about her physical attractiveness. Be reassuring and don't tease her about physical imperfections. Love her unconditionally for who she is.

6. Her libido may be wavering. Try to be as supportive as possible and not use blame for any problems that you may be experiencing. Women, like men, suffer from lower testosterone levels during this time of life. Using a testosterone supplement might help restore libido as well as energy levels. Suggest that she find a physician who is knowledgeable in testosterone therapy for menopausal women. Offer to join her for a couple's visit to the physician so you can learn more about her change of life and how you can help.

7. Many women experience a new sense of self. Embrace the positive changes and honor her menopausal wisdom without fear.

Acknowledge Your Private Fears

I'll always remember Alisse, a 47-year-old patient I had taken care of for over a decade who had made an urgent appointment to see me one morning. A CPA with her own business, she had always impressed me as a tough, nonemotional kind of gal. This particular morning she was anything but her typical self.

"I just had to get in to see you as soon as possible."

I was anticipating some form of emergency situation such as unusual bleeding, shortness of breath, chest pain, or some equivalent. I was not prepared for her next comment.

"It's the banner ad!" she shrieked.

"What banner ad?" I shrieked back.

"I was surfing the Net, reading the *New York Times* morning news, when this flashing banner ad almost made me fall off my chair."

My curiosity was beyond restraint. "What did it say?" I shouted as if I were at a hometown football game.

"It said: 'Uncomfortable sex doesn't have to be a part of menopause. . . . Click here.' I clicked and it was an ad for a vaginal lubricant designed for menopausal women. It was as if they were reading my mind. My boyfriend and I had just had sex last night and it was almost intolerable. I felt so dry and so embarrassed that I couldn't say anything. Ever since I've been going through these changes it's been getting worse, but I've been afraid to admit it to either myself or to him. And there it was, flashing in my face this morning—for the whole world to see. I couldn't believe it."

I reassured Alisse that a condition so popular as to merit a banner ad on the World Wide Web was something she shouldn't be ashamed of. I examined her and diagnosed atrophic vaginitis, a condition caused by estrogen deficiency that results in drying and thinning of the vaginal tissues. Fortunately, the treatment was easy and straight-forward and the results would be almost immediate relief. She was pleased that this secret fear could be cured so readily. Her reluctance to discuss this problem up until now made me wonder how many of us hold private fears related to midlife changes that might be ruining our quality of life. Do we need some banner ad equivalency to stir us into action? Do we prefer to suffer in silence rather than seek an appropriate solution?

Private Fears of Midlife Couples

For some women, avoiding sex altogether becomes a solution to dealing with atrophic vaginitis. Not understanding that this is a condition related to estrogen deficiency, causing decreased vaginal lubrication, some women think it is a sign of old age and would rather give up sex because of the pain than admit that there is a problem. A man may not be aware of the condition and may even start to blame himself for his partner's discomfort. The secret fear quickly becomes an obstacle to the relationship.

Likewise, a man may be experiencing difficulties achieving a firm erection. His private fear is that he is becoming impotent. In reality, this is a normal physiological change in response to lower testosterone levels. His fear goes into overdrive that he won't be able to perform and soon enough he starts to avoid sex with his partner altogether. If he was able to discuss the change, he would learn that a bit more physical stimulation or direct pressure on the penis should cure the problem. What might be even worse is if he believes that his problem is caused by his lack of arousal from his partner and he tries to get a hormone boost by having sex outside of his committed relationship. This form of self-therapy might have disastrous consequences for the relationship.

Being able to acknowledge and discuss private fears with your partner should be considered essential preventive therapy for the male and female midlife passage. If you are not comfortable discussing your fears directly with your partner, bring them up with your physician at the time of your exam. This is a great opportunity to be proactive in your own health care.

Invite your partner to attend so the questions can be thoroughly and professionally answered. According to the renowned sexologist Dr. William Masters, the "privilege of exchanging vulnerabilities" is the essence of good communication in a relationship. If you can't be vulnerable with your loved one, you should ask yourself why not?

Some questions my patients commonly ask about their private fears:

• "If I don't use it, will I lose it?" Lack of sexual activity will make sexual intercourse more difficult, but not irreversibly so, over time. Vaginal atrophy (thinning of the vaginal tissues) can set in and the vagina may shrink to a smaller size. For the man, prolonged lack of sexual intercourse may inhibit sexual function in the future.

• "My sexual appetite is not the same as it used to be. Is there anything that can be done?" Libido can definitely change for both men and women as we transition through the hormonal changes of our 40s, 50s, 60s, and 70s. Low sex drive is not abnormal and can be successfully treated with varying techniques. The most important recommendation is to have a thorough physical exam and history taken by a qualified physician who is familiar with sexuality issues. Before you make your appointment, inquire if your physician is experienced in helping patients with hormonal and/or libido problems. If the answer is no, ask for a referral or consult with a local university medical center for an appropriate recommendation.

• "I'm afraid I'm losing my energy. What can I do?" Lack of energy at midlife can be a symptom of many different conditions. A thorough medical exam, including a complete physical, history, and laboratory blood work, is necessary. Evaluating your diet and exercise program is also key. Are there signs of thyroid or other hormone deficiency? Are there underlying medical conditions, such as heart disease, anemia, diabetes, or even an occult malignancy? Is there an element of depression? Sometimes it takes energy to make energy, and ramping up your exercise regime may be appropriate. Perhaps vitamins and a dietary overhaul are also in order. Whatever the cause, it is important not to ignore changes in energy levels or assume that getting older is the reason.

• "I'm afraid my partner is having an affair. What should I do?" Open communication, not confrontation, is the key. Share your fears and ask if they are justified. Be prepared to accept whatever the answer may be, knowing it could be painful. If your suspicions are correct, decide in advance if the situation is salvageable and if hope and trust can ever be restored. If you are overwhelmed or confused, seek professional counseling as soon as possible to sort things out.

There may be opportunity to build from the ashes. It all depends upon the willingness of both parties. If your suspicions are refuted, ask yourself what makes you think your mate is having an affair? Can you trust your partner? Are your suspicions still justified or are you insecure within yourself that your partner might leave you for another? Are you worried about your own sexual appeal or physical attractiveness? Being brutally honest with ourselves about our own insecurities is never easy.

Are changes in your partner's libido or sexual activity causing you to worry about infidelity? Discussing these issues with your mate is critical—before they lead to worse problems. Seeking medical or professional advice might be beneficial for both of you.

• "I'm afraid to admit I'm getting older." Our attitude about aging will ultimately affect how we navigate our later years. If we see only the negative side to growing older, we will cheat ourselves of what could become the best years of our lives.

What is your perspective? What is your partner's? Who are your role models? We are not following in the footsteps of our parents' menopause and andropause; our generation is breaking new ground. With age comes wisdom, maturity, and the freedom to be in tune with your own ideals. Embrace your advanced degree in living and enjoy new opportunities.

As Oliver Wendell Holmes Sr. summed up his philosophy, "We don't stop playing because we grow old, we grow old because we stop playing." Other inspirational thoughts on aging: "I promise to keep on living as though I expected to live forever. Nobody grows old by merely living a number of years. People grow old by deserting their ideals. Years may wrinkle the skin, but to give up wrinkles the soul" (General Douglas MacArthur). "Some men never seem to grow old. Always active in thought, always ready to adopt new ideas, they are never chargeable with foggyism. Satisfied, yet ever dissatisfied, settled, yet ever unsettled, they always enjoy the best of what is, are the first to find the best of what will be" (William Shakespeare).

• "I'm afraid of looking old." Our perceptions of looking old have changed over time. Chances are, if you compare what you look like now to a picture of your mother at the same age, you will look substantially younger. We have learned how to take better care of ourselves over time. There is no reason to walk stooped over at age 60 if we have been taking care to prevent osteoporosis through exercise, diet, and hormone management. Likewise, we need not look wrinkled and shriveled if we have protected our skin from the damaging effects of the sun's rays and stopped polluting ourselves with nicotine fumes if we were smokers. Keeping well hydrated (at least eight 8-ounce glasses of water a day) is also essential. And the most critical aspect of not looking (or feeling) old is to maintain a healthy and active lifestyle. This does not mean we all have to prepare for marathons on a regular basis, although there are plenty of 50-, 60-, and 70-year-olds who do. It does mean we have to prioritize exercise—at least 30 minutes daily of aerobics and two to three times per week of strength training. By prioritize I mean not letting exercise fall to the least important item on the to-do list for the day. This will not only make you feel younger, it will keep you looking substantially younger than your years. (More about the benefits of fitness and exercise in Chapter 11, "The Truth about Anti-Aging.")

Moving from Fear to Greater Intimacy

"Deep and thorough . . . most private or personal . . . very close and familiar"—these are terms used to describe what it is like to be intimate with a partner. The flip side of intimacy is intimidation. This is what happens to men and women at midlife. We tend to intimidate ourselves with our own repressed fears and vulnerabilities, thus blocking our path to greater intimacy with our partner. By harvesting the emotional energies at midlife, we can unlock our hidden desire to develop even deeper avenues of intimacy. We can move from crisis point to turning point.

Intimacy is about connection, communication, friendship, and trust. It involves a larger presence than merely sexual involvement or sexual intimacy. Psychological predictors of long-term marital satisfaction and success have shown that intimacy is the most significant factor. Passion takes second place to intimacy, which should not be surprising. The flame of passion may diminish over time, perhaps in response to natural hormone declines, but the foundation of intimacy keeps a marriage healthy and intact.

"I can't recall the last time we both hit the sack at the same time," my 49-year-old patient Roz was lamenting during her annual exam. "It's amazing to me that we've been married for the past twenty-two years and it's probably been close to a year that we've actually put our heads on the pillow at the same time, kissed each other good-night, or snuggled at bedtime. We still have sex, from time to time—that is, if we get up in the morning and don't feel too rushed. But something is missing. And I didn't even think about this, Doc, until you asked about bedtime. No one has ever asked before."

"Well, it's not a typical question doctors ask their adult patients,"

I replied, "but it should be asked." I then proceed to get to the heart (and soul) of the matter. "Who typically goes to bed first?" I asked. "And what does the other partner do during that time?"

Roz was quick to respond. "Phil *always* comes to bed later. He claims he's not tired when I am, around 11:00 P.M., and he's typically on the computer playing bridge with someone halfway 'round the globe or surfing the Net. I've gotten so used to it, it's part of the routine. I don't even wake up anymore when he hauls himself into bed, around 1:00 or 2:00 A.M. If I do wake up later, it's because he starts to snore."

"What happens in the morning?" I continued to probe gently.

"Usually I get up early to let the dogs out and he sleeps later," Roz recalled. "I might come back to bed for more snooze time if it's the weekend, otherwise I'm out the door headed for the gym. By the time I return home, he's usually up working in the home office or back on the computer."

Like a good detective, I needed to collect my background data first. Roz was complaining about a loss of sexual interest, and so was her husband. Although Phil hadn't come to this office visit—I typically encourage the partners of my perimenopausal and menopausal patients to come along—I was putting together the pieces of the puzzle. Since Roz had recently turned 49 she was worried that her hormones were lacking and this could be the problem. I listened carefully and took her concerns into account.

"Certainly," I explained to Roz, "your hormones may be contributing something to the problem, and I'll do some blood tests to check them out. However, I think there is something we can fix first."

Roz looked at me with complete amazement. "Is there something you found wrong on my exam?"

I quickly reassured her. "Your exam was perfect; it's your bedtime situation that needs some fixing."

She looked at me with bewilderment. "What do you mean, Doc?"

"Well, do you remember how you described your routine at night, with you and Phil coming to bed separately, night after night, at completely different times? You even mentioned 'something was missing.' "

Roz nodded her head in agreement.

"What is happening, Roz, can definitely be fixed. But you have to be willing to make some changes, and so does Phil. First off, you are both cheating yourselves out of one of the most valuable parts of being married."

"What do you mean?" Roz asked incredulously.

"Each time you go to sleep in your bed, alone, without your partner by your side, you are each missing out on the magic of comfort intimacy. It doesn't have to be about sex. It's about the security and comfort of having your soul mate by your side, without the distractions of the outside world. By synchronizing your bedtime, you actually line up your circadian rhythms and become more in harmony with each other. Going to bed together does wonders for your communication, not to mention your love life. Just the snuggle factor alone is worth it. The other benefits will follow. It can only help your relationship. Unless Phil prefers his relationship with his computer, he needs to give this a try."

"But what if he's not tired?" Roz inquired, prepared for the possible objections.

"Tell him it's not about being physically tired, it's about intimacy, physically reconnecting and synchronizing your biorhythms. The two of you will reconnect in more ways than one. Please give it a one-month trial. Come back with Phil for the next visit and we'll reevaluate."

Forty days later Roz and Phil came to the office. I reviewed Roz's hormone test results. Her FSH was slightly elevated, meaning she had started into her perimenopausal state. However, her estrogen and testosterone levels were still within the normal range and she was still having monthly periods. I did not feel hormone replacement was necessary at this time. Before I could say more, Phil interrupted.

"Doc, I have to admit I was not keen on being told to change my bedtime habits. But it was the best thing that ever happened to us. I had no idea how we got into that vicious cycle, but we definitely were drifting apart. Who would have guessed such a simple change could make such a huge difference? And it's helped our sex life a whole bunch, too."

Roz agreed. "We feel a lot closer now. And not just that. Phil has more energy in the morning since he doesn't go to bed as late. Now the two of us can go off to the gym together or get out for a morning jog. He's also lost some weight and doesn't seem to snore as much— or at least I don't notice it. Anyway, things are much better."

I was thrilled to hear about their success. This was a case of replenishing intimacy on a daily basis. It's not always enough to get your daily dose of vitamins, calcium, exercise, or hormones, although all these certainly help. Look at yourself in the mirror and ask, "Have I had my dose of intimacy today?" If not, find ways to revive what had been a part of your loving relationship. Intimacy, like love, requires work—it needs to be tended to regularly.

Determine Your Relationship IQ (Intimacy Quotient)

Use this survey as a guide to determine your relationship IQ (intimacy quotient). Unlike hormone levels, there are no blood tests available to give precise answers as to whether your relationship is deficient in the intimacy department. However, maintaining a certain level of intimacy is critical to the health of your midlife relationship.

1. I feel comfortable confiding my fears to my partner.
2. My partner shares his innermost thoughts with me.
3. We share planning fun events.
4. We frequently laugh together.
5. We can go out to dinner and enjoy each other's company, with or without friends.
6. We look forward to doing things together.

7. I make my partner a top priority in my life.

8. My partner makes me feel that I am a top priority in his life.

9. I appreciate my partner's interests, even when they are different from mine.

10. We share the same bedtime most nights of the week.

11. When physically apart, we still communicate daily.

12. We share a similar value system.

13. When I talk with my partner, I feel he is truly listening.

14. When I talk with my partner, I feel he understands what I am communicating.

15. When my partner talks with me, I listen closely.

16. When my partner talks with me, I understand his message.

17. My partner and I look forward to time alone together.

18. I consider my partner to be my best friend.

19. I feel my partner considers me to be his best friend.

20. I feel as close to my partner now, if not closer, than when we first fell in love.

21. I believe my partner feels as close to me now, if not closer, than when we first fell in love.

22. My partner would be the first person I would confide in if I had a serious health problem.

23. I believe if my partner had a serious health problem I would be the first person he would confide in.

24. I always keep my partner's confidences to myself.

25. I trust my partner to keep my confidences private.

26. I unconditionally trust my partner.

27. My partner unconditionally trusts me.

28. I feel my partner appreciates me, and I let my partner know how much I appreciate him.

29. When disagreements arise, we both can feel comfortable expressing our opinions.

30. I feel comfortable sharing this survey with my partner.

Multiply each true answer by 5.

SCORE 125 or greater: The two of you are true soul mates. You could be role models for other couples.

100–124: The two of you are definitely on the same wavelength. Keep up the good work and keep those lines of communication open.

75–99: Most of the time you are on the right track, but your intimacy issues need tender loving care and constant surveillance. Look for opportunities to enhance your intimacy.

Less than 75: Your relationship needs a boost in this area. Make a conscious decision to prioritize the intimate zone and reap the benefits. Some practical guidelines follow.

Reclaiming Your Capacity for Intimacy: Seven Critical Strategies

Make a Conscious Decision to Reconnect

Both men and women have greater needs for emotional intimacy at midlife than at any other time of life. From a hormonal, physical, and psychological perspective, this is a time of significant vulnerability. Hormonal levels are fluctuating and receptors throughout the body, including the higher neuroreceptors in the brain controlling rational thought and emotions, have altered in sensitivity. This is the time to reach out to each other rather than pull away. "At middle age the soul should be opening up like a rose, not closing up like a cabbage" (John Andrew Holmes).

When children grow up, become independent, and move away, there is often an emotional void that may be felt deep within our core. This can affect men as much as women. I will always remember being at parents' orientation for our older daughter before she left for college. A psychologist addressed the audience, which consisted mainly of 40- to 60-year-old baby boomers. His message was, "Be prepared for the emotional changes even if this is not your first or only child to go away." A 50-something well-dressed and slightly graying father stood up and, with tears in his eyes, bravely confessed, "Nobody told me it would be this hard." His wife reached up to give his hand a gentle squeeze. I looked around and saw a fair share of moist eyes in the room. Hankies were flowing freely—and it was not just the women who needed them.

A man or woman may also feel a void, especially after retirement. The positive reinforcement of being productive or being needed at work is gone. Even if you or your partner has been looking forward to retirement, there is a new emotional space to be filled. All those years of work made work a centerpiece of personal identity. With the end of work, there is an adjustment in ego. Being present for each other emotionally and sharing your feelings during this key transition is essential to nurturing intimacy.

Appreciate Your Partner

Sometimes this is easier said than done. Too often we become so familiar with each other that it seems unnecessary to say or show what we believe the other should already know. "Obviously, we've lived together this long; she knows I appreciate her," said Ned, a 62-year-old retired stockbroker, who wondered why his wife of 30 years harbored resentments.

Vera's resentments had grown to the point where she couldn't even express her frustrations to her husband. "She just seems angry all the time," Ned noted. He was right about that but didn't realize that chronically forgetting her birthday or their anniversary, or never giving her a compliment from time to time, made her feel unvalued and unloved.

My father passed away at age 87; his death was just one week short of his sixtieth wedding anniversary. At the funeral, my mother, through tears, confided that not one day passed that he didn't thank her for her love and the care that she gave him. "I kept telling him, 'Ben, you don't have to thank me; I'm your wife,' but he thanked me anyway." I was very moved by this revelation. Although I had not heard my father publicly profess his appreciation to my mother, this was truly a showing of love and a sign of the intimacy that kept them together all those years.

Share and show your appreciation, before it's too late. Your partner is not a mind reader and you both can't always presume to appreciate each other because of the duration of your togetherness. Lack of appreciation translates to lack of caring and creates a giant void in intimacy. It opens a window for someone else to jump through who can willingly show appreciation for what the withholding partner cannot or will not express. Sometimes a midlife affair can innocently start because someone else was there (usually younger) who could appreciate the unappreciated spouse.

Treat Your Spouse As a Friend

How often do you confide intimate details about yourself, your life, your kids, or even your spouse to your friend? That's what good friends are for. By definition, a friend is an ally as well as a supporter and a good sympathizer. We feel confident that we can trust our friends. We are bonded by the comfortable exchange of mutual caring.

Friendship is vital to lasting marital relationships as well. Research has revealed that friendship with one's spouse is the most significant predictor of a happy and successful marriage. But, you may ask, "Doesn't being married mean you are friends?" Not necessarily. In the beginning of most male-female relationships, an element of friendship is established. How this component is maintained becomes quite a different story. Over time, the critical elements of friendship may become replaced with daily duties of making a go of practical living. The marital relationship becomes more of a steady to-do list than the workings of a vital friendship. Too often spouses turn to outside friends for the support and camaraderie they are lacking in their own marriage. Outside friends are important, but it is even more important to maintain the element of fun and friendship within the marriage. How can we do this?

Use your relationship with your best friend (outside of your spouse) as an example. Lisa and Natalie are best friends. All of a sudden Lisa no longer has even 10 or 15 minutes a day to chat on the phone to keep in touch with Natalie. They stop making plans to do fun things together. Neither is putting in the effort to keep the relationship going. It's not surprising that the friendship part of the relationship quickly erodes.

What would happen to your friendship with your spouse if neither of you made plans to have fun together or spend quiet time together or share your innermost thoughts? Just like everything else that seems to be worthwhile in life, friendship requires effort. It is not a given that comes with the marital vows. Friends don't take friends for granted; neither should marital partners. Make dates with each other. Give each other surprises. And by all means find ways to have fun with each other.

Be Sensitive to Each Other's Needs

While it may seem overly simplistic, being tuned in to your partner's needs is a basic prerequisite for strengthening intimacy. Sometimes we are so wrapped up in our own daily existence, especially when faced with midlife worries, that we lose sight of our partner's parallel concerns.

Sarah was so worried about developing age spots and facial lines that she was oblivious to Lance's concerns about his hair loss. He would drop hints such as "You know Huxley, the guy down the block? He just had a hair transplant. What do you think of that?"

"Not much. I didn't really notice it," was Sarah's casual response. Lance thought that meant she wasn't even noticing him since it didn't seem to register that he was going through the same thing as their neighbor. When it was pointed out to Sarah later that Lance thought she was being insensitive, she admitted to being so wrapped up in her own needs that she really wasn't aware of Lance's concern. Rather, she thought Lance was being insensitive—he should have known she was having bad hot flashes when she constantly had to beg him to turn on the air conditioner in the car. Each partner's needs and vulnerabilities were below the other's radar zone.

During midlife, we need to be especially sensitive and tuned in. Listen with empathy and understanding. Educate yourself about what changes your partner might be experiencing. Ask, delicately, what his or her special concerns or desires are and what you might do to help. Better to be an overly caring spouse than a haphazardly insensitive one.

Get Rid of Old Anger and Resentment

Continuing to harbor old grievances serves to erode intimacy. Midlife is a time of rebuilding and moving forward to a higher level. If we look at this as a transition time not only for ourselves but for our relationship, we can free ourselves of toxic baggage. If past resentment keeps surfacing, it blocks our growth for a closer bond. If we envision midlife as a time to remodel, we can rid ourselves of clutter and move on to a fresh start. Acknowledging emotions and using them constructively to open clear channels of communication is key to fortifying relationships. Sometimes it helps to write down the old grievances on scraps of paper and burn them in a bonfire on a full moonlit evening. From the ashes will grow a new, and more fulfilling, relationship. Who knows, you may even start a new tradition of having romantic bonfires when the moon is full.

Let There Be Space

While togetherness is good, too much of a good thing can be bad. At midlife, there is a delicate balance between being together and being apart. It is not reasonable or wise for couples to be constantly in each other's presence. Too much togetherness can be stifling to a midlife marriage.

When 68-year-old Jack retired from his real estate business, it was a major change for him not to have an office to go to every morning. He and his wife, Ruth, thought he would enjoy doing some consulting work from his home office. This would give them more time together and more leisure. Little did either of them realize that this seemingly simple change would jeopardize their 35-year marriage.

"I really thought I would like having Jack around home more often after he retired," Ruth recalled wistfully. "But in reality it turned into something of a disaster for both of us. I didn't quite realize how much I enjoyed having the house to myself in the middle of the day. I was used to the peace and quiet and getting the things done that I needed to accomplish. I don't mean to seem selfish or petty, but after Jack was home for three weeks in a row, I got fed up with daily lunch duty and not having the freedom I was used to. If I had a friend who wanted to do something with me in the day, I felt guilty about leaving Jack at home by himself. I know it sounds silly, but our total togetherness almost destroyed us.

"But the good news is, we came up with a solution. Jack was also getting restless being in the house all day—this wasn't the routine he was looking forward to. So he decided to join the community center which had a gym. Every midmorning he leaves the house now and works out at the gym. He then showers and catches a light lunch at the deli or meets a friend or two. This is perfect. I get my freedom again and he gets his workout. When we join up again at five for cocktails, we get to share our experiences. It's much more fun this way."

The moral of this story: Don't stifle each other with togetherness. Leave enough loving space for intimacy.

Practice Random Acts of Affection

Think back to your early days of courting. What was your relationship like? Can you remember how you met? How did you express your affection for each other? It's time to jar your memory, because intimacy is fueled not so much by passion as by small and consistent acts of affection.

Too often as our relationship ripens, not only do we settle into routines, but we "forget" to be affectionate with each other. When one partner continually lags behind, it becomes difficult for the other to keep up a one-person show. Soon, even the affectionate partner loses the motivation to be affectionate. The good news is, renewing affections can become a self-fulfilling prophecy. Don't just sit there waiting for affection to come to you, go out and practice one random act of affection daily.

Here are some hints:

• Give your partner a coupon book for a Massage-of-the-Week Club. Have one massage on a tear-off page for each week of the month—for example, "Good for one foot massage," "Good for one scalp massage," "Good for one back massage," "Good for one facial massage." Be creative—use your imagination. This could be habit forming.

• Prepare a bubble bath for your partner. Dim the lights and set out candles.

• Find a photo of the two of you during your courtship period. Hide it in an unlikely spot such as the medicine chest or refrigerator. Watch for the reaction.

• Mail a surprise love note—just for the heck of it.

• Send flowers—for no particular occasion other than it's "I Love You" Day.

Warning: Be prepared for results. You'll be subject to random acts of affection in return—and more intimacy.

CHAPTER 7

A Woman's Guide to Surviving Her Man's Midlife Change

It was Monday morning and I was rushing about as usual. There always seems to be a jolt on Monday mornings as my family transitions from the relative ease of weekend flexibility to the rigid reality of Monday-to-Friday schedules. This particular Monday appeared to be typical.

I was preparing for a full day at my office practice followed by an evening lecture I was to deliver, titled "Hormonal Changes through the Ages." I was thinking about the title and how relevant it was to the hormonal milieu that was brewing under my very own roof. In just our household alone we had several real-life case studies representing every hormonal category. My husband and I were in our mid-40s, each experiencing our own unique version of midlife transition; our two older kids (one son and one daughter) were in blatant late adolescence at the ripe ages of 17 and 18; and our youngest was a mere 9-year-old prepubescent girl. Then there was the extended family living a short distance away—my postmenopausal parents in their late 70s with their own set of hormonal challenges. How refreshing, I mused, to speak on a topic so close to home and one that I had a professional passion for.

I was suddenly jarred from my morning daydreaming by the incessant ringing of the phone. The answering machine hadn't picked up because it was the back line that was demanding to be answered. The dreaded back line—it was supposed to be used only for emergencies, unless it was a kid's friend who somehow had the secret number and was too impatient to wait for the front line. I grabbed the phone. "Hello, this is Dr. Cetel. Can I help you?" I asked, not knowing what awaited me on the other end. It was a familiar voice.

My husband, Joe, was calling. He was on his way to the airport and he was explaining that he had run into a bit of trouble. "Would you be kind enough," he asked with an unusual sweetness in his voice, "to call the conference organizers to say that I think I will be running late."

Joe is also a physician who lectures on medical topics. That morning he was running off to catch a plane to Chicago, where he was presenting a lecture on gastrointestinal disease at a medical convention. Being a gastroenterologist with a sense of humor, he was known as Dr. G.I. Joe.

"Well, dear," I inquired innocently enough, "what kind of trouble have you run into?" He proceeded to explain that he was calling from his car phone. He was literally stuck in his car (a Z3 BMW—more about the car later), which was at that very moment lodged under the rear of a 16-wheel diesel truck, which apparently didn't see him when they were both turning right at the traffic signal. His tone was that of someone who had merely been in a fender bender and here he was waiting for the Jaws of Life to extract him. I could hardly believe what I was hearing. "Are you all right?" I shrieked into the receiver. Talk about the male denial factor!

"I'll be fine," he insisted. "Could you please just call the conference and let them know I'll be late? We'll talk later."

I checked his files and found the phone number for the conference in Chicago. I immediately called the conference organizer. "I'm calling on behalf of Dr. Joe Weiss. Unfortunately, I don't think he'll be able to give his presentation. He's had a bit of an accident on the way to the airport." I spared them the details. "He won't be able to catch his flight on time. Would it be okay for him to reschedule?" I don't recall what the exact response was other than they were terribly sorry to hear about his accident and wished him well. The back line was now ringing again.

"Good news!" Joe exclaimed on the other end of the line. "The Jaws of Life are here and they think they'll have me out in forty-five minutes. The paramedics are here, too. The bad news is they're insisting on taking me to Mercy Hospital. I'm afraid I'm not going to make it to the conference after all. Could you call them back to let them know?" he asked sheepishly.

"I can't believe you've just had a near-death experience and all you're concerned about is your conference. Of course I've called them and I've already let them know you won't be coming. I'm just so glad you're alive and talking! I'm coming down to the hospital right now, and by the way, please thank the paramedics for me." I was exasperated and relieved at the same time. I felt like a mother who had caught her child doing something dangerous and naughty, wanting to reprimand the child and at the same time wanting to sweep him up in my arms and hug him forever. I knew where these feelings were coming from.

The drive down to the hospital seemed to take forever. I was quite familiar with the route, but this drive had an eerie uneasiness to it. I was rushing to see my husband. I wasn't a doctor going to the hospital to see an admitted patient, I was a wife coming to see a husband with unknown injuries. My mind was soaring. My emotions were running the gamut. I felt unconditional love, mixed with anxiety but seasoned with a dash of anger. The anger made me feel guilty, but it was there and I had to face it.

All I could think of was how grateful I was that he was alive and how angry I was that he was actually driving that BMW. It definitely had not been my decision to get the sports car. It had become a symbol of my husband's own midlife challenge. One day, sometime shortly before Joe's forty-fifth birthday, he announced that he really liked the new Z3. I actually thought he was joking because he knew I would always give examples of the warning signs of male midlife crisis and lecture about middle-aged men running around in hot sports cars trying to regain lost youth. I would acknowledge to the audience that it was a better alternative to running around after young frolicsome females half their age. It always got a laugh.

But today I wasn't laughing. I was on my way to the hospital and lamenting that this midlife crisis business could really be dangerous to your health. I was also upset with myself. Why, I asked myself, had I let him get that car in the first place? Here is a six-foot three-inch man squeezing into a sports car half his size—not to mention that he had to keep the top down so his head wouldn't rub the roof. Hey, but that was half the fun. I'm just five foot six and I felt the car was too small for me. But at the time, I thought I was just being a surly midlife wife. I knew when to back off, and I did. We even joked about it. Since the car was featured in a James Bond movie, we dubbed it the 007 car and got license plates aptly personalized as "Uh Oh 7."

When I got to the hospital, Joe was being wheeled into the MRI to see what organs, if any, were damaged. The highway patrol officer was there in the emergency room filling out his report. "Ma'am, are you his wife?"

"Yes, can you please tell me what happened?" I tried not to sound too hysterical.

"Well, when you're in a car the size of an ant, sometimes a big Mack truck won't see you. Usually the Mack truck wins. Your husband is a lucky guy. You probably don't want to see the car though, ma'am. It's totally totaled. It'll turn your stomach. We had to use the Jaws of Life to get him out. The steel frame was crushed within a fraction of an inch of his head and neck. It's amazing he's talking. We got a laugh out of the license plate though. That's a good one. Uh Oh Seven, I'll remember it."

I thanked the officer for his help and waited outside of the MRI scanner. There was some good news. The radiologist, a friend and colleague of mine, came out. "Everything looks fine inside, although there is some swelling around the vertebrae in the neck. We'll have to observe him in the hospital for at least a few days." I was eternally grateful that his physical injuries were limited.

Joe emerged from the MRI scanning room, a collar around his neck, still dressed in formal lecture shirt, tie slightly askew, and small bits of glistening glass protruding from his cheeks. He had forgotten to mention the windshield had shattered on top of him. "What a way to start the week" he joked.

Fortunately, Joe recovered well, without any permanent scars. His ego was a bit bruised though. We talked about what had happened and, without laying blame, agreed that Uh Oh 7 would not be replaced. Perhaps this was a big wake-up call. The crash symbolized a warning light about midlife madness, rushing around and not taking the time to smell the roses and count your blessings. In some ways, this crisis was a turning point. It made us both poignantly aware of how much we love and appreciate each other for who we are. A new sports car was no longer an essential ingredient of life. We both survived our midlife crisis and consequently developed new strengths. Fortunately, not all midlife crises need be as dramatic to make a point.

Turning point message: Try to see the good message even in times of crisis. Don't wait for disaster to strike before appreciating life's blessings and those you love. Beware of midlife sports cars, motorcycles, or other dangerous toys. (Submessage: Watch out for big midlife men in pint-sized sport cars.)

Hemorrhoids, Hernias, and Hypochondriacs

"When Arthur turned fifty-eight, it was as if his warranty had completely expired. I mean he acts as if he's falling apart." June, an attractive 53-year-old, lamented about her husband's seemingly deteriorating state of health.

"Well, what medical problems does he actually have?" I asked.

"He's been diagnosed with a hernia; that's been bothering him for some time. He also has hemorrhoids, but he's too embarrassed to do anything about them. And last, but not least, whenever he hears about someone else having a medical problem, he begins to think he has one, too. I'm afraid he's turning into one of those hypochondriacs or something. Is there anything I can do to help him, Doc?"

"You could help by setting the example, which you are actually doing already. By taking care of yourself, you are showing by your actions that this is the time of life to be proactive. Encourage him to get off his hemorrhoids and go in for a good physical checkup. The hernia is not life-threatening but probably bothers him every day. He needs to get it fixed. Then he can start living again."

Men in particular are reluctant to take care of themselves. They either deny that they have problems or worry about the problems they are afraid of getting. In particular, some men view midlife as the beginning of the end and always see the glass half empty. Show your partner that the glass is really more than half full, and that it has bubbly champagne. Encourage him to get on with his life, fix his minor physical problems, and allow his mind to be free. Sometimes the woman has to set the example, or even make the appointment for her mate. If making the appointment seems too bold, help him out by doing the research, finding the best specialist for his problems and giving him the phone number and address. Show him you care by taking a positive step.

Turning point message: Recognize that your partner needs help. He's afraid of getting old and sick. Reaffirm your love and desire for him. Rather than cajole him, lead by example. If that isn't enough, do some basic research to make it easy for him to help himself. (Submessage: Whining, complaining, and or cajoling will not inspire him.)

Something Strange Happens at Forty

"I don't know how to describe it, but I just felt different when I turned forty. I know it sounds crazy, but I was getting these adolescent feelings on the inside, but when I looked in the mirror my body was telling me something else. My temples were graying, my hairline was receding, and I was starting to get that dreaded gut. Things were changing with my body, but what was going on in my mind was even scarier," Bruce said, describing what his life was like 12 years ago, before his divorce and before his second marriage to a woman 10 years his junior. He is now in his 50s, fully gray, slimmer, and the father of two sons, four-year-old Bobby and two-month-old Eric.

He continued: "I knew I was in trouble when I started to get feelings for a woman at work. They were kidlike emotions. I wanted to go out with her. That really frightened me. My first wife and I had been married for seventeen years and I had never even thought about cheating on her. I felt like time was passing me by and I needed to do something or else it would be too late. As a matter of fact, she was the first one I told about this. She got scared and didn't know how to handle me. At the time, I had no clue what was happening. If I knew then what I know now, it might have saved my marriage. I thought I was alone and that no other guy ever had thoughts like that. If only someone had told me I was going through some kind of midlife phase, I think we might have worked it out. I don't blame my wife for the divorce. I know I'm wiser now and would love to spare other guys the grief I went through. If only I had known that there was something about turning forty that can make a guy feel and act so strange."

Turning point message: Some men need reassurance that turning 40 isn't the end of the road. Take steps to help your man feel better about himself emotionally and physically. (Submessage: Puberty doesn't last forever, nor does male midlife transition.)

What's Going On with Dad?

It seemed to flare up overnight. At least that's what it seemed like to Harriet when 51-year-old Peter, her husband of 25 years, father of their two sons, and former school board trustee, flipped out. "I think that when Tim went away to college, something just kind of snapped in Peter's head," Harriet said. "There also was the death of Peter's longtime associate Ralph; he was in his late fifties and just had one heart attack—his first and final." Harriet was trying to analyze the inexplicable. There were no words to describe how she felt. Peter was having an affair with their housekeeper and the two of them moved out of the house together.

Harriet's counselor reassured her. This was Peter's problem and definitely not Harriet's fault. "This is so hard to accept. It's so unlike him," Harriet said in despair. "He's always been a great dad. I admit we've had our tiffs, but nothing ever major—nothing that should merit this kind of behavior. I'm at a complete loss." Harriet was grasping for any bit of insight the counselor might offer to help her understand and cope with her husband's bizarre behavior. The hardest part was trying unsuccessfully to reassure her sons when they kept asking, "What's going on with Dad?" There were no explanations as far as she could tell.

The counselor tried to put it in perspective. Peter was a man who on the surface seemed to be content, a good father, and a reliable husband. All of a sudden he starts to act completely out of character. "This really didn't come out of nowhere, it came from within. You see, Peter didn't plan on turning unpredictable. He was already giving you hints that he wasn't quite satisfied with his life. He would get up in the morning, squint at himself in the mirror, and make remarks like 'Do I really look that bad? Gee, I'm getting old. I hate wearing reading glasses. It really bothers me that my golf swing isn't as strong as it used to be.' These were hints of his discontent with himself."

"But I never told him he looked bad or seemed older," Harriet retorted defensively. "I guess I never told him that I thought he was still wonderful either."

"Now please don't blame yourself. He provided his own self-loathing, and his actions were meant for you to loathe him as well. Of course he didn't think of all the consequences either. Teenage boys and midlife men in particular never think things through thoroughly. When they are caught, they are sometimes remorseful, but not always. He may even want to blame you for his unrest because it's easier than faulting himself." The counselor took a long breath and looked deep into Harriet's red, tearful eyes. "You know he was acting out his anger and frustration—at himself and the world in general. When his friend died, it hit him as hard as a sledgehammer that 'there but for the grace of God go I.' All of a sudden not only does he feel like he's getting old, he sees one of his own dropping dead. It's a heavy dose of reality—too much at once. It comes at the time of life when he is most vulnerable. He's experiencing hormonal changes just like you are, but he probably doesn't even realize what's normal and what's not. And then when your older daughter goes off to college, perhaps he is feeling, 'I need to flee the coop also.' You have to keep in mind that he isn't deliberately trying to hurt you, Harriet. He truly doesn't understand what he's doing. He knows something is missing in his life, something is wrong. He's searching for answers—in all the wrong places—and trying to seize his lost youth."

"Yes, but doesn't he know he's making a fool of himself?" Harriet asked, regaining her composure.

"No. He's oblivious to what other people think. Many midlife men are able to justify their actions to themselves. He may feel confused but doesn't think of himself as an idiot. He's feeling emotions he hasn't felt before. His occasional impotence doesn't help either. By running off with forbidden fruit, he's trying to get a hormone boost as well. Chances are the affair won't last long. It's hard to say who he's hurting more—himself, or you and the kids."

"Well, I think this whole male menopause thing stinks. Couldn't he just take some hormone replacement like I do and get over it?" Harriet was letting her deep hurt generate some anger.

This is good, her counselor thought. *We need to get some anger out here.* The counselor then said, "Actually a checkup and a hormone evaluation wouldn't be a bad idea if he's willing to go. I can give you the name of a doctor who specializes in this. But don't count on a single magic pill to give a quick fix. There could be many layers here."

Harriet felt some relief. Maybe there was still some hope, and perhaps some answers as well. "In the meantime," she wondered, "what can I do to survive this?"

How to Survive Your Husband's Midlife Affair

1. Decide if you still want him in your life. This is a completely personal and individual decision. It will take a lot of healing and time to restore the trust. If you succeed, you may enter a place of even greater closeness. Some couples do come out stronger. For some, the affair represents the ultimate turning point in the relationship. For others it is the point of no return. I definitely do not recommend waiting for an affair to be an excuse for therapy. Better to take preventive measures and try counseling first.

2. This is the most important time to develop yourself as an independent person. Even if he is unwilling to seek counseling, get some for yourself. It will prepare you to cope with your own emotions during this stressful period.

3. Keep in mind that it won't last forever. There will be life after the affair. And time does heal.

4. Make plans for yourself. Don't put yourself on hold waiting for him to sort things out. Start creating your own life. Do things with friends or by yourself.

5. Take up a new hobby or join a continuing education class. Get out of the house.

6. Don't retaliate with an affair of your own.

7. Learn to depend on yourself, not him.

8. Don't whine, beg, or make idle threats.

9. Accept that this is his problem and not your fault.

10. Surround yourself with loving and supportive friends and family.

Turning point message: The affair is his problem and not your fault. Decide if you still want him in your life. Make your own plans. Seek counseling and let your own inner strength blossom. (Submessage: Learn to depend on yourself, not him.)

When Men Won't Talk: The Unspeakable Symptom

"If only men could talk, it would help us women out a whole lot," said Connie, a 60-year-old new patient, referring to her 63-year-old husband, Cliff. Since this was my first time seeing Connie as a patient, I had never had the opportunity of meeting her husband. I explained my office policy that husbands are always welcome and even encouraged to come along for the visit, as long as the patient feels comfortable with it.

"Well, that would have been helpful a few years ago when we were all puzzled about Cliff's behavior."

I was intrigued and needed to know more. "Did Cliff have some type of unusual condition?" I inquired, always eager to hear about a good medical mystery.

"Yes and no. It depends on what you mean by unusual. Let me explain what was going on. Cliff and I have been married for forty years now. He was always a quiet guy. But then again, most of the men I know, at least from my generation, are not known for sharing their feelings or doing too much talking. So being quiet, or closed, as some of my friends would say, wasn't at all unusual. And I'm the kind of wife who could do enough talking for the both of us. I guess you could say we were a good match that way."

"Is Cliff getting medical treatment now?" I asked.

"Thank goodness, yes. He's a different person now. When I was first going through my change of life I admit I got a bit moody. But I came out of it after I started getting a good night's sleep again, thanks to the hormones. I thought Cliff was kind of upset with me. He just seemed to have an angry edge about him. He didn't sleep well and just about everything upset him. When I tried to talk to him, he said there was nothing wrong and he didn't want to talk. So I left him alone. The more I left him alone, the more he wanted to be alone. And then he started sleeping later and later. It finally dawned on me that something was wrong."

Connie continued: "Since Cliff wouldn't leave the house, I had to get a doctor to make a house call. I couldn't believe it when the doctor said he was depressed. I always thought depression meant crying or being weepy. I didn't realize that when a man gets depressed he can get snarly. And since he wasn't good at expressing himself, I didn't know he was having that kind of emotional problem. The doctor said it was his change of life that threw him into it. Cliff was worried about getting old, seeing me have my menopause, and he just shut down the little emotion he had. Thank goodness for antidepressants. He still doesn't talk a lot, but at least he's back to being himself. I'll bring him along on the next visit."

What Every Woman Should Know about Male Midlife Depression

1. Depression is the most common problem associated with male midlife crisis.

2. From an early age, men are taught to control their emotions by hiding them.

3. A man typically won't admit to being depressed, even if he is showing a depressed mood.

4. Depression is typically underdiagnosed in men and overdiagnosed in women.

5. Feelings of sexual inadequacy can trigger depression in a man.

6. Excess irritability and moodiness may be signs of depression in a man, whereas weepiness or emotional outbursts are more characteristic of depression in a woman.

7. Attempts to self-medicate with alcohol or drugs may signal an underlying depression.

8. Sleeping excessively or having difficulty sleeping can be warning signs.

9. A depressed spouse may have a difficult time making decisions or enjoying his former activities.

10. Men have a higher rate of suicide than women.

11. Depression in a man is treatable; the difficulty lies with the diagnosis.

12. Counseling can speed recovery.

13. Regular exercise, even moderate walking on a daily basis, can help combat mild depression.

14. Men have a higher risk of depression when their testosterone levels are too low.

Turning point message: Depression in a midlife male is not uncommon, but it can be difficult to diagnose. Once recognized, depression can and should be treated. Relationships improve significantly when the depressed spouse is successfully treated. Regular exercise can help improve mild depression. (Submessage: If you think he's depressed, you're probably right. Don't count on him to be the one to recognize it. Recommend treatment as soon as possible. Waiting too long can jeopardize physical and mental health as well as a midlife relationship.)

Navigating Your Mate's Midlife Crisis

Women have all the advantages here. We have been well schooled in menopausal mind-set. By the time we arrive at menopause, we have acquired advanced placement credits. After all, menopause is preceded by a good 10 years of perimenopause transition where the typical woman has many opportunities for hot flashes and other menopauselike dress rehearsals. We know that menopause is real and we are ready to take it on.

Men, on the other hand, have no such advantage. They have not had the benefit of a periandropausal prep course to hone their skills. Their health care providers may be trying to catch up with the medical literature, scratching their heads and asking, "Is there really such a thing as andropause?" All the while, every eight seconds of every day a new man enters his midlife phase. Ready or not, here he comes. Because we are the women functioning as the significant other in the relationship, it behooves us to step up to the plate. What should we do?

Be aware and tuned in to his midlife changes, even if he's not. But give him space. Be sensitive, caring, and understanding. If there seems to be something bothering him, be supportive and encourage him to open up and discuss it. If there are sexual problems, don't bring them up while you are both in bed—he may feel threatened. Talk about the situation on less sensitive turf. This is the time to reaffirm your love and affection for him. His feelings are just as vulnerable as yours, and his fragile male ego may need some extra strokes at this time of life. Look for some of the more common signs of male midlife transition. His passage will be more gradual than yours and his symptoms may not be as apparent. However, if he does not anticipate the very real physical and psychological changes that do occur, he may be in for an extra rocky transition.

What Changes Should I Be Watching For?

The most common sexual and genito-urinary symptoms include reduced libido, diminished erections, less ejaculatory volume, and a less forceful urinary stream. This could be very upsetting to a man as it is a direct signal of aging and diminished sexual capacity. These symptoms can have a domino effect and cause irritability, depression, and anger. An undertone of male angst can develop.

A depressed middle-aged man often shows anger and irritability more often than a sad or mournful affect. His energy levels may diminish because of sleep disturbances and hot flashes or as a consequence of depression. He may have a reduced sense of well-being and heightened fears about aging. To make matters worse, he may deny all of the above because he has been trained by society that real men don't reveal weaknesses. Denial is a man's worst enemy. You need to be the gentle support staff and the voice of reason.

This is the time to encourage him to have a thorough physical exam. Ask him to do it for your sake since you love him. You might even help him set the appointment. Thank him for being willing to go. All men need extra encouragement in this department. We women have far more experience in the doctor's office, having experienced annual exams and prenatal visits in the past.

Beyond the Medical and Technical

How you as his lover, spouse, and partner handle his midlife journey will have a far greater impact than a single prescription of Viagra or testosterone. Healthy doses of love, friendship, and respect must be present. Developing a mutual understanding of each other's transition is key.

Men are trained to hide their emotions and to deal with the situation. At midlife, emotions tend to rise to the surface. Recognizing this is important for both of you. He may refuse to go to counseling, but that doesn't mean you shouldn't, in order to cope with your own feelings.

Realize that the mind and the body are intimately connected. Try to exercise your body and encourage him to do the same. Even if you have not done so before, this is the perfect time in life to start exercising together. Even if you just walk 30 minutes a day, that's 30 minutes of time together complete with benefits for your mind and body.

Think about dating again—that is, dating each other. Renewing the friendship aspect of the relationship can be fun. Plan a surprise each week—a dinner out together, a movie, a date at a cappuccino bar. Be imaginative—he'll appreciate the effort. Reaffirm your love and consciously prioritize your relationship. You can't change what may be going on within your mate, but you can bring him and your relationship to a better place.

CHAPTER 8

A Man's Guide to Surviving
His Woman's Midlife Change

Somewhere between the ages of 40 and 50, your spouse's hormonal circuitry shifts gears. Slowly, surely, the biological clock is winding down and the reproductive juices of the ovary are preparing for retirement. As ovulation slows and becomes irregular, so might her menses. With the gradual loss of estrogen, she may start to experience some of the signs and symptoms of menopause, even though she is not technically in menopause yet. This 5- to 10-year prelude to menopause is referred to as *perimenopause*. This is the stage where a woman can take stock of her health, reduce her risk factors, and maximize the quality of the rest of her life. It is the taste of things to come. She may or may not be prepared for it. Just as you will have shifts in your hormones, moods, and physical state, so will she. No matter what her stage of readiness, you and your mate will have an infinitely better transition time if you are tuned in, mentally aware, knowledgeable, and emotionally available.

Dealing with Perimenopause

Perimenopause is not a new invention designed to intimidate men. It is a description of the hormonal changes occurring in the years prior to the onset of menopause while a woman is still having periods and may still be fertile from time to time. Dr. Rogerio Lobo, in his definitive medical text *Treatment of the Post-Menopausal Woman*, defines perimenopause as a "complex time in a woman's life, during which unpredictable and wide fluctuations in ovarian function and their physiologic consequences occur. A greater understanding of this physiologic event in women is warranted, as are how women perceive of these changes and what treatments should be considered."

It is not often that a respected medical researcher uses adjectives such as *complex* and *unpredictable* in one sentence to describe a life transition that all women go through. As a medical researcher and one who reads between the lines, I interpret this definition as one that comes with a disclaimer: Beware—we don't yet have the full handle on this hormonal phase. As a woman and as a physician with a particular interest in this time of life, I recommend that my readers (the men in particular) not run for the hills with misgivings when their women hit age 40. However, a good understanding of what is happening up front—that is, on the surface and in your face—and behind the scenes (the physiological changes) will vastly improve the quality of life for you and your mate.

A Hormone Meltdown

When 42-year-old Janice came to see me for a "third opinion," she admitted she was at her wit's end. A tall, striking brunette, she looked the picture of perfect health. She said she had been happily married for 18 years to a "trooper of a husband" with whom she had two teenage daughters who were "just great kids." She worked full-time as an accountant and for the most part enjoyed her work. With such an ideal background I was beginning to wonder what problems, if any, she could possibly be experiencing.

Janice then collapsed into tears. She had been referred to me because two other physicians had already told her there was nothing wrong with her at all, that it must be emotional issues and perhaps what she really needed was a psychiatrist. She said she would be willing to see a shrink if that's what the problem was, but deep inside she felt there was something more physical involved. She had heard about me through other friends and hoped I could help.

After a thorough physical exam, I asked Janice to get dressed and come back to talk with me in the office. I assured her that I valued her own intuition and we would discover what was happening. I asked her to describe what her main problems were and her biggest fears.

"Well, to begin with," Janice said, taking a big breath, "I do think I am more sensitive and edgy than I used to be. But here's the thing: it doesn't happen all the time. I can be perfect for two weeks and all of a sudden this mood will come over me. My kids never know what to expect. I won't be able to sleep well at night—sometimes I actually wake up and I'm covered with sweat. I feel tired, draggy, and boy, oh boy, stay out of my path, because when the shadow sets in, I can be vicious. I feel sorry for my husband. Our sex life is miserable, especially with this vaginal dryness. Then there's another thing: I get these migraine-type headaches just about the same time. And sometimes, I feel so fuzzy-headed that it's hard to concentrate at work. Last week I went home early two days in a row, which is not like me."

"Anything else?" I prompted. "What about your sex life?"

"No one has asked me about that before. But the truth is, I have less and less interest in sex. It's as if my sex drive has driven off. I can't even talk about it with my husband. I'm too embarrassed. When I went to the other doctors they told me I was healthy and everything was fine. But I know something is wrong. When I asked them if it could be menopause, one laughed and said I was way too young and the other said that, because I was still getting my periods, it was impossible to be in menopause. He did take a blood test to check a hormone level and said it came out normal. Doc, do you think I need a shrink?"

I reassured Janice that I didn't think she was going crazy. "In fact," I reassured her, "what you are describing is not uncommon for women in your age group." I could see the tension visibly melt from her body. She was obviously relieved to hear that I didn't think she was losing her mind. "But I will need you to do a bit of homework for me. Please keep track of your symptoms on this calendar for the next twelve weeks and come back so we can evaluate it. But promise not to give up in the meantime."

Janice returned in three months and we reviewed her symptoms together. Her menstrual periods were becoming irregular. Instead of the usual 28- to 30-day cycle she had been experiencing, her periods were now 35 to 45 days apart. And the bleeding was becoming heavier. When we looked over the calendar it became clear that two weeks before her period, not only would her mood deteriorate, but she was getting frequent "warm spells," sleep disturbances, headaches, and night sweats. It became more difficult to concentrate during this time and she had no sexual desire at all.

We reviewed her blood work and hormone levels. It was clear that Janice was suffering from perimenopausal symptoms caused by changing levels of estrogen and progesterone. Her body was no longer ovulating on a regular basis. Her night sweats, sleep disturbances, and premenstrual headaches were the result of greatly reduced estrogen levels. So was her vaginal dryness. The imbalance in the hormones was also making her moody. No wonder she was losing her sex drive as well. Her perimenopause symptoms differed from PMS (premenstrual syndrome) because of the prominence of hot flashes and sleep disturbances—all signs of estrogen deficiency.

We talked about her lifestyle and options for treatment. To begin with I recommended starting on a regular exercise routine. With Janice's busy schedule, exercise had fallen off the priority list. I suggested that she make more time for exercise by having her husband Todd help out with more of the to-do list items. He would reap the benefits by having a happier, healthier wife as well. When Todd accompanied Janice for the next follow-up, he was already eagerly pitching in. We also discussed adding soy products to Janice's diet as a natural means of putting more estrogen into her system. Vitamin E supplementation was also recommended.

Because Janice was having irregular bleeding and had not been using an effective method of birth control, I recommended a very-low-dose birth control pill as a means of controlling her cycles, providing effective contraception, and providing a better hormone balance throughout the month. Unfortunately, women in their 40s have the highest rate of abortions for unwanted pregnancies (next to unwed teenage girls) presumably due to surprise late-in-life pregnancies. Also, it was not too long ago that hysterectomies were being performed almost routinely on women in their 40s for irregular vaginal bleeding. Now with the low-dose birth control pill providing good cycle control, many of these hysterectomies can be avoided. I also asked Janice to continue monitoring her symptoms for the next two months and to keep a diary to see what else might be triggering her hot flashes.

Janice returned as a new woman. "I feel I'm my good old self again," she reported. "No more night sweats, the hot flashes and vaginal dryness are gone, and so are those miserable headaches. My period on the pill is light and definitely predictable. Our sex life has improved considerably. The exercise is giving me more energy and I can treat my family the way they deserve to be treated. Thanks for rescuing me from my hormone meltdown."

I was thrilled for Janice that her sense of self, as well as her sense of humor, was back. Todd and the girls were also delighted.

How to Know If It's Perimenopause

The symptoms of perimenopause may resemble other conditions or medical problems. It is recommended that your partner have a thorough physical exam and appointment with her physician for a full diagnosis.

Use the following questionnaire as a general guide to determine if your partner is experiencing perimenopausal symptoms. Please answer yes or no for each item.

1. My partner is between the ages of 40 and 50.
2. Her periods are still regular.
3. She has stopped menstruating for close to a year.
4. Her periods are becoming irregular.
5. She has sleep disturbances.
6. From time to time she has hot flashes and/or night sweats.
7. She has more anxiety, especially the week or two before her period.
8. Her sex drive is waning.
9. She is skipping periods.
10. Sometimes she has trouble concentrating.

If your answered yes to all questions except 2 and 3, chances are your partner is entering perimenopause. If her cycles have stopped completely for close to a year, she may already be in menopause. If her periods are still regular and normal, she may or may not be entering perimenopause. By being aware of the physical and emotional changes of this time of life, you can be more supportive of her needs. The fact that you are aware and caring will provide an instant benefit. Most women who struggle through this time of life feel that their spouse just doesn't understand what they're going through. Congratulations for taking this step and becoming a more sympathetic and knowledgeable helpmate.

How to Help Your Partner Get through Perimenopause

1. Let her know that you are aware of what happens to a woman during this time of life. Encourage her to share her feelings, needs,

and wants with you. Let her know you are there and available. Polish up on your listening skills.

2. Ask her if she has noticed any changes in her cycle or her physical state and suggest that she keep track of her symptoms in a diary to facilitate reviewing symptoms with her. By keeping track of her cycle, you will both be able to know at what point her symptoms seem to be strongest and you'll be better prepared. For example, if her estrogen levels are low starting two weeks prior to her period, she may be more prone to hot flashes and sleep disturbances. By noting what may provoke the hot flashes, such as hot drinks, stressful situations, warm clothes, or being with certain people, she may try to adapt her environment and avoid those apparent triggers. You may help by offering her a cool refreshing drink or turning on the air conditioner (without being asked) when she is warm and helping to defer stress when possible. Your caring and understanding will have incredible benefits for both of you. The calendar will be a useful resource for her physician as well.

3. Support her in finding a physician who is knowledgeable and sensitive about perimenopausal issues. A recent study of 438 Australian women looked specifically at the symptoms related to perimenopause. The women were closely followed for menopause-related symptoms over a seven-year time frame. Most intriguing was the finding that the women experienced the greatest change in menopause-related symptoms during the transition between early and late perimenopause. These symptoms included hot flashes, night sweats, and vaginal dryness. Many women consult their physicians during this time of life with similar problems and are often told they are too young to be going through the change. This study confirms the fact that many women do experience menopausal-type symptoms even though they are not officially in menopause.

For many years I have seen frustrated patients like Janice who were suffering and could not receive adequate treatment. If your partner's physician doesn't understand what she is experiencing at this time of life and why, it is time for a change. Recommend that she call in advance and ask if the doctor she intends to see is familiar with perimenopause. If not, it's time to move on. He or she might have been wonderful at delivering babies, but if your mate's physician isn't ready for her next stage of life, find one who is.

4. Accompany her to the doctor's appointment. Your presence will validate her concerns and you'll learn more about what treatment options are available.

5. Be extra patient and kind. Practice random acts of kindness. Treat her to a massage or other form of relaxation.

6. Take up healthy hobbies together. A daily 30-minute walk together does wonders for communication as well as aerobic capacity.

7. Talk about what happens in the bedroom—but not when you're in the bedroom. A difference in sexual appetite is one of the most common areas of imbalance between couples. This can become particularly difficult at midlife, especially for the woman. Her hormonal changes are more dramatic than the man's. Vaginal dryness can also be a culprit, making sexual intercourse less desirable and even painful. Fortunately, there are products available that can help, and you both should be aware of this. Over-the-counter products include Replens and Astroglide, which are non-hormone-containing lubricants. Some women benefit from vaginal creams that contain a small amount of the female hormone estrogen. The estrogen will strengthen weakened vaginal tissues and make intercourse more comfortable.

However, many couples find that the true culprit isn't lack of sex, it's lack of communication. You need to understand what's on her mind and she needs to understand how you feel. Often, after years of marriage or togetherness, couples settle for a routine. The routine may be satisfactory for one or perhaps neither of you. Just because you are used to something doesn't mean it's the best option. But sometimes couples persist in carrying on tradition because they are fearful of making a change and just don't know what is really going on inside their beloved's brain. She may want and need more cuddling or gentle touches or even a gentle back massage. Forgetting or shortchanging foreplay can have negative consequences for the harmony of the relationship. And don't forget about the wonders of affection, inside as well as outside of the bedroom.

8. Suggest that one of you use a barrier method of contraception if she does not use very-low-dose birth control pills and you are still fertile.

9. Appreciate her for who she is. Be generous with honest compliments. Often at perimenopause, women become more vulnerable and sensitive about their physical appearance. They are fearful of looking older, putting on weight, and not being as attractive to their mates. They may take extra time getting ready or fretting about perceived imperfections. This is where you as her knight in shining armor step forward. Don't wait for her to ask, "Do you think I look good in this outfit?" Tell her that you think she looks beautiful.

One husband once told me in front of his wife that he no longer needed to let her know that he found her attractive. "After all," he said with conviction, "we've been married this long and there are some things you don't have to talk about because I know that she knows that I still find her attractive." His wife, Beth, and I gave each other grimacing looks.

"Do you enjoy hearing nice things about yourself?" I asked Dave.

"Yes, but—" Dave started to say before I cut him off.

"There really is no 'but' here other than to pay attention and not get lazy or sloppy with terms of endearment or appreciation for each other. Not giving a well-deserved compliment should carry some marital penalty."

My words sunk in.

Dave turned to Beth and said, "I always find you attractive. I just took it for granted that you knew."

The look of joy on Beth's face was beyond description. As they embraced, I left the room thinking, "This is better than any prescription med."

10. Help her maintain her energy levels with regular exercise, regular sleep (at least seven hours), and healthful eating. Offer to help out with chores so she has the time to exercise. Smoking leads to early-onset menopause. Encourage her to quit smoking if you haven't already.

Five mini-meals per day are the best way to beat hunger and keep blood sugar and energy levels balanced. Weight gain is not a necessity if she balances exercise with healthful eating. Putting on weight is a very sensitive issue at this time of life. Be as helpful as possible by showing her your support and love. Refrain from joking about weight issues, even if you think it is harmless teasing.

Encourage her to try soy products. They can help keep hot flashes away and may also be good for maintaining healthy cholesterol levels.

Encourage her to use calcium supplements and weight training to maintain her bone density.

11. Look for stress-reduction techniques to help her get more centered and to lessen anxiety. Having an understanding partner who helps with domestic chores is especially important during this time of life. Help her make private and quiet time for herself. Consider yoga for relaxation and flexibility. Even reading a good book by herself for at least 30 minutes can be beneficial for the serenity of her mind. We function better with a calm mind, and the fuzzy-headed feelings tend to subside when we are less stressed.

12. If hot flashes are waking her up at night or wreaking havoc in her life, consider herbal remedies as well as very-low-dose hormone supplementation. Vitamin E, an antioxidant, has been recommended to soothe hot flashes and protect the heart. It is antiquated thinking to presume that she has to wait until she is engulfed in complete menopause before she can do something about her hot flashes. Make sure she checks with her physician.

13. Consider suggesting that she go on a women's retreat or get away for a weekend with women friends. The female companionship can be uplifting and spiritually fulfilling. It will reinforce for her who she is as a person and not just a mom, wife, or career woman. She needs to know and honor herself as a person. Getting away on a men's retreat is a good idea for yourself as well.

Turning Fifty Is a Sensitive Issue

For most women, celebrating a fiftieth birthday is a landmark event. Fifty truly symbolizes the epicenter of midlife. Fifty also is close to the average age (50.5 years) at which most women step over the threshold of perimenopause and enter the domain of menopause. Natural menopause is traditionally defined as the time period that occurs after a woman has missed her period for 12 consecutive months. She is no longer fertile. The ovarian factories no longer produce delicate bundles of estrogen, progesterone, or even testosterone. Her entire body has had a hormonal wind-down and is facing the next stage. Estrogen, the dominant female hormone, plays a significant role in the function and efficiency of many organ systems and is responsible for many of the physical attributes of being feminine. Estrogen also affects a woman's emotions as well as certain cognitive abilities. Although scientists and clinicians have not yet mastered a full understanding of all the complexities of this magnificent hormone and its total effect on the female mind and body during menopause, there is enough knowledge to help you peacefully navigate your partner's change of life.

What Every Man Should Know about His Partner's Menopause

1. Every woman's experience of menopause is unique.

2. The most common physical symptom of menopause is the hot flash. Approximately 85 percent of women experience some form of

heat sensation during menopause. However, not all hot flashes are created equal. They can range from subtle warm-glow feelings from time to time, to just feeling warmer in general, to intense heat evoking hot flashes that leave a woman drenched in perspiration. Sometimes heart palpitations, anxiety, feelings of doom, and/or sleep disturbances can accompany the hot flashes. Some hot flashes are triggered by certain events while others are spontaneous. Hot weather or an overly warm room may lower the hot flash threshold. Be sensitive to your partner's reactions to heat or hot climates.

Fifty-three-year-old Mary felt guilty about telling her husband, Desmond, she just couldn't stand another summer in the desert. Although Desmond loved golf and didn't appear to be affected by the 90 degree–plus temperatures in Arizona, he could see that Mary would fall apart in the desert. He couldn't understand why she wouldn't join him on the golf course or why she was irritable all the time. Only after Mary gathered the courage to explain that her menopause made her especially sensitive to heat did he finally get it. "Why didn't you tell me sooner?" he asked after their second season in the desert. "I didn't want to spoil your enjoyment," Mary replied. "And I thought you would know about these things." Because she suffered in silence, Mary's hot flashes and resentments only became worse with time. Fortunately, when she was able at last to discuss what was bothering her, they both started to enjoy their summers in the more temperate San Diego climate, where Mary can join Desmond on the golf course as well.

3. Moodiness and irritability are often related to the psychotropic (mood-altering) effects of estrogen depletion in the brain. A specific example of estrogen's impact on mood occurs when a woman experiences frequent sleep disturbances. The lack of estrogen causes hot flashes that disrupt a woman's REM (rapid eye movement) dream time. Over time she may become chronically sleep deprived. It has also been shown that REM sleep is critical to psychological well-being. Even if your partner thinks she had a full

night's sleep, she may wake up feeling groggy. Chronic sleep deprivation can turn into fuzzy thinking, forgetfulness, irritability and anxiety. This is certainly frightening for her, worrisome for you, and aggravating to your relationship. Now that you are aware of this potential syndrome, you can be an even better partner by observing her sleep pattern. She may be completely unaware that she is sleeping fitfully. If you are able to observe her sleep and notice if it is particularly restless, discuss it with her and show that you care enough to suggest that she get help. A good night's sleep can make an enormous improvement in her well-being and your peace of mind.

Lack of estrogen can also directly affect feelings of well-being. There is scientific evidence showing a correlation with estrogen levels and mood. The old joke "I'm out of estrogen and I have a credit card so you better watch out" brings the mood and sensitivity issues to the home front.

4. Most women in menopause experience some form of vaginal dryness. Be aware and sensitive to this condition. Suggest creative ways to overcome it. Be playful in applying vaginal lubrication. Ask her about her comfort level. She may be too embarrassed, self-conscious, or afraid of hurting your feelings to let you know that sex has become painful.

5. Lack of estrogen in the vaginal region can also cause reduced blood flow to the vaginal tissues. During arousal there is less engorgement of the surrounding tissues and this can interfere with stimulation and orgasm. Some women even develop a lack of sensitivity in the clitoral region. Certain touches that used to cause excitement now may be unpleasant or uncomfortable, and some women even develop an aversion to sexual touching. Typically estrogen can reverse these changes, so it is worthwhile to get a medical opinion about treatment. Specific vaginal forms of estrogen are available, such as Estring (Pharmacia & Upjohn) or Vagifem (Pharmacia & Upjohn), where there is only minimal absorption of estrogen by the body.

Sometimes a woman's lack of excitement is misinterpreted by her male partner as a rejection of him as a lover. Often there is a physiological cause that can be cured. Once a couple understand this, they experience tremendous relief.

6. Help her sex drive. There is a cartoon showing a middle-aged couple going out to dinner. The husband asks, "Why do we need candles on the table? We don't need to be romantic—we've been married long enough now." Libido problems are not just hormonally based. This is a time of life where your partner may be even more appreciative of attention paid to romantic details. Many women not only feel they are losing their physical attractiveness but that their romantic and emotional needs are neglected at menopause. What is a comfortable routine for the male partner may become dull or unappealing for the woman. This is the time of life to go out of your way to rejuvenate your romantic skills and show that you appreciate her for who and what she is. Hormones can help libido, but a healthy and vital relationship is the most critical ingredient.

I'll never forget the day my 59-year-old patient Inez came in for her annual exam. Just a few days shy of her sixtieth birthday, she seemed to be particularly anxious. I asked how things were going at home and in particular if there were any new concerns or problems. She said her hormone therapy was keeping the hot flashes away and in general she felt in good health. But then after a long silence, in a hushed and saddened voice, she whispered, "Felix and I are not getting along well." I was about to ask more about her 32-year marriage when I discovered what appeared to be a genital wart on one of her labia. I needed to let her know that she had contracted a sexually transmitted disease and that we would have to do more tests. I wondered what this information would do to her already shaky relationship if she knew Felix had been unfaithful.

"Inez," I said as I started to break the news, "I'm seeing something on your pelvic exam that's new. It's a genital wart and—"

Before I could say another word, Inez broke out in tears. "I'm so ashamed of myself. I never would have had the affair with Hugh if Felix had been more attentive and understanding."

I had made the wrong presumption. Midlife men aren't the only ones to have affairs. However, when a woman has an extramarital relation at midlife, more often it's for emotional need rather than sexual fulfillment. A midlife man may seek a hormone boost or reassurance about his virility by having an affair. A midlife woman is typically looking to fill an emotional void in her life.

Inez tried to explain her actions: "On the outside, we looked like a happily married couple. On the inside, Felix was the 'happily' part and I was just the 'married' part. I guess I was just looking for someone to fill the void between us."

7. A woman may feel more empowered at menopause. As more women are entering the menopausal years and are living longer lives, a desire may be born to seize the day. No longer content to be identified as just "my kids' mom" or "my husband's wife," women are exploring new roles and new options. The subtle shift in hormone balance from estrogen dominance to a slightly higher ratio of male hormone may also have some behavioral impact.

8. Culturally, our society has shifted dramatically from the grandmotherly image of the menopausal woman of the 1950s to one of idolizing the "I've arrived" role model portrayed by such menopausal icons as Lauren Hutton, Jane Fonda, and Goldie Hawn. Clearly today's 50-year-old woman is not living her mother's menopause. Best to acknowledge this change and not treat your partner as just somebody's mother or grandmother.

What Every Woman Wishes Her Man Knew about Making the Menopause Easier

1. Please don't feel obliged to try to fix my problems. I need you more as a good listener than a fixer-upper. Listening and understand-

ing is far more important than trying to solve every problem. Giving me your support is a true gift.

2. If I'm moody from time to time, please don't take it personally and please don't get angry. Showing some extra love, appreciation, and tenderness at this time would be wonderful.

3. When we have time together, please be in the moment with me. It's hard to talk to you if you're reading the paper, going through the mail, or glancing at the television, even if you feel you can hear everything I say. Hearing is not the same as feeling and communicating. More than ever before, this is the time when we both need to be more in touch with each other.

4. Let me know that I'm still loved. Don't wait until I have to ask, "Do you still love me?" Sometimes you take it for granted that I should know that you love me, but it will never insult me to hear it from your lips.

5. I may be doubting my physical attractiveness. Let me know that you still appreciate the way I look. Compliments are never hurtful. A simple remark, "You look wonderful in that dress tonight," can rekindle fond feelings and restore confidence.

6. Let me know that I'm still important to you. Don't assume that I know this already.

7. Please take my feelings seriously. Joking about a few extra pounds that I might have put on can be more hurtful than you might think. It's not that I don't have a sense of humor, but there are certain subjects that may trigger hurtful feelings.

8. Please make me feel that I, not your dog or your golf clubs, am your number one love.

9. Please keep yourself as healthy and in the best shape possible. It's more important now than ever before for both of us.

10. Making me feel sexy is about more than sex. Help me get in the mood. A hefty dose of affection, love, and respect will have better results than a bottle full of Viagra.

11. Spend at least half an hour of together time with me each day. Look into my eyes and let me know I'm still special in your life. I'd love to do the same for you as well.

The next section explores techniques to enhance harmonious relationships, invigorate midlife sexuality, and maximize robust longevity. You'll learn strategies to help fortify you and your partner's physical selves, empower your emotional selves, and rediscover the heart and soul of what it means to be a couple in love.

PART III

GETTING TO HORMONAL HARMONY

CHAPTER 9

Midlife Romance

romantic—inclined to dream of adventure, heroism or love; imaginative but impractical; of love or a love affair

love—intense affection or warm feeling for another
American Heritage Dictionary

It's a fact of life: as individuals, we are living longer and staying in better shape, both physically and mentally, than any of our ancestors. But what about the long-term health of our relationships? As life expectancy is increasing, divorce expectancy is following suit. Approximately 50 percent of long-term marriages disintegrate, without either partner having a real understanding of when and where things went wrong. Sometimes a void becomes apparent after a major change in lifestyle or a life-altering event ushers in a wake-up call. Retirement, empty-nest syndrome, or death of a parent, friend, or colleague leads to a reevaluation of our priorities. Sometimes there is emotional pain, especially if we wake up to discover that our relationship is not what we had anticipated. These wake-up moments are a normal part of midlife maturation, as in "wake up and smell the roses."

Too often, in the haste of day-to-day modern living, we may not even notice the roses, let alone take the time to inhale their sensual aroma. When we do slow down to indulge our senses, we can appreciate what we have missed and ask ourselves why we don't partake more often. So, too, with midlife and the nurturing of mature love. Romance provides the opportunity to rekindle the sensual spirit of a relationship. This is based upon commitment, affection, and devotion. Romance also recaptures the essence of what it is like to know true love.

In reference to the previous definitions, it might be easier to relate to the term "romantic" if we view our midlife journey as an adventure, see our partner as our hero or heroine, and continue to pursue our dreams while nurturing our love for each other. At midlife, all the correct ingredients are in place. Sometimes they just need to be stirred up to get maximum flavor. *Midlife romance* doesn't have to be an oxymoron.

The Chemistry of It All

A courtship begins when a man whispers sweet nothings
and ends when he says nothing sweet.

Anonymous

On the surface, romance appears to be combustion of wild, intoxicating, fleeting, feel-good passion that works its way into an emotional state called love. Dive beneath the surface and what we discover cascading through the rapids of the bloodstream and literally being pumped from the inner chambers of the heart is the essence of pure love, those microscopic couriers of emotions, our hormones. Indeed, romance and love are physiological states with profound repercussions on our mood, mentality, creativity, energy, and even our health and longevity. These chemical messengers of emotions traverse the blood-brain barrier and activate neurological synapses with electrifying results. At midlife, our hormonal systems are primed and eager for just this sort of activation.

Igniting Our Midlife Love Hormones

If we think back to our first experience of falling in love, it is not hard to recall the unique blend of energy and exhilaration that resulted in a near-euphoric state. Indeed, our heart may be racing, our palms sweaty, and our senses in a state of peak sensitivity. When two people are attracted to each other and by each other, a virtual frenzy of hormone and neurochemical activity occurs. Our natural high is fueled by the release of hormones, neurochemicals, and endorphins, the body's own opiate system. The more we bond with the object of our affection, the more opiate particles are released. Love can be addicting, but this is just the beginning.

Being held in our lover's arms, or even touched by the object of our affection, causes a gush of oxytocin, a potent bonding hormone secreted by the pituitary gland. Couples entering into the state of love tend to float, almost immune from the worries of the world. In reality, the immune system does get an overall boost from a shot of love.

In the woman, oxytocin works in synergy with estrogen and is directly involved in the forceful uterine contractions necessary for labor and delivery. After the baby is born, oxytocin plays a critical role in milk letdown in the breasts and reinforces the bonding between infant and mother. During nursing, the release of oxytocin results in pleasurable and relaxing sensations for the mother as even more of this magical hormone is released. In response to the cry of her baby (or even the cry of another baby), oxytocin is automatically secreted from the pituitary, causing the breasts to leak or even spurt milk. In essence, oxytocin becomes a remote control of mother-infant bonding to the highest degree. So too with touch. The more the mother touches or is touched by her baby, the greater the release of this marvelous hormone.

In a similar manner, oxytocin promotes bonding between a man and a woman through touch. Just as a woman's breasts are sensitized by the release of this hormone in response to a baby's cry or touch, so too is there a response to her partner's touch. Hand holding, cuddling, snuggling, hugging, or even being in the proximity of her lover can cause the release of oxytocin. By increasing desire and arousal, there is also enhanced bonding between the partners. The sensitization can be so great that even the sound of a lover's voice, the scent of his particular pheromone (subtle scent that can attract the opposite sex) or even a certain look can trigger oxytocin release. The more hormone, the greater the chance of touching; the more contact, the greater the release of hormone.

If we choose not to touch, or not to spend time with our mate, oxytocin levels will fall and the bonding cycle will unravel. Emotions do play a role in our ultimate decisions, but our hormones help jump-start our physiological responses. Long-distance relationships as well as relationships that are void of touch can be hormonally challenging. The good news is that they can also be salvageable by making the choice and by reinstating the art of touch.

Scientific studies have shown that touch deprivation can have significant consequences on human life. Babies who are raised without physical affection are more likely to have difficulties with social skills, personality disorders, and less ability to express affection as adults. As we grow older, our need for touch and physical intimacy does not wane. Couples who stop hugging, snuggling, stroking, or even just holding each other have a higher chance of depression, sleep disturbances, reduced immunity, irritability, anxiety, and the *D* word: divorce.

In a survey of prominent divorce attorneys, "Lawyers on Love" by Andrew Taber (May 5, 2001), *Men's Health* magazine listed the lack of nonsexual touch as one of the top 10 reasons midlife couples divorce. "Married men tend to touch their wives only when they're looking for sex. Lawyers say that's a mistake. Men underestimate the power of nonsexual touch. Women who come to an attorney looking for a divorce often talk about how their husbands no longer hold their hands or offer unsolicited kisses and back rubs—all things that make women emotionally connected." Men benefit from the healing effects of touch as well. Touch is an undeniably potent resource. When was the last time you gave your significant other a good old-fashioned hug? It just may be time to get the oxytocin pumping again.

What Do Love, Romance, Infatuation, and Chocolate Have in Common?

If you answered "calories and Valentine's Day," give yourself part credit. If your response was "phenylethylamine," congratulations— you deserve a jumbo box of chocolates and a double-strength hug to go. Phenylethylamine, or PEA, a naturally occurring form of amphetamine that our own body produces, has affectionately been referred to as the "love molecule." Coincidentally, chocolate, the all-time favorite of Valentine's Day gifts, contains large amounts of PEA as well. So it appears that tradition, if not pure instinct, has led lovers to offer each other molecules of love, disguised in fat-laden morsels of edible ecstasy. In fact, Americans invest over $600 million on chocolate gifts for Valentine's Day alone. The good news is that chocolate may be as beneficial for the physical heart as it is for the romantic heart. Recent studies have shown chocolate to be rich in polyphenol antioxidants, which can increase the level of circulating HDL cholesterol (the good cholesterol) and perhaps reduce the risk of heart disease as well.

When a couple first fall in love, there is an initial outpouring of PEA from the brain as well as the release of dopamine and norepinephrine. When the neurotransmitter dopamine is secreted, it helps us feel good and leads us to pursue more pleasure. Dopamine paves the way for an emotional high, while norepinephrine stimulates the adrenaline rush. The combination of these natural substances is quite powerful, potentially addictive, completely natural, and can lead to physiological bonding. Perhaps love can be viewed as a form of adrenaline rush that is also supplemented by the sex steroid hormones, estrogen and testosterone.

As a man's testosterone flourishes, so does his PEA. Similarly, as a woman's estrogen level peaks just prior to ovulation at midcycle, so does PEA. It is not unusual for a man or a woman to be flush with love and actually have flushed skin, increased heart rate, and heavier breathing. Not surprisingly, PEA levels spike to higher levels with orgasm. Perhaps to prevent physiological overdrive, the body protects itself over time by developing a tolerance to the effects of phenylethylamine. The heightened intensity of new love is slowly exchanged for a relationship characterized by deeper bonding and commitment. The release of endorphins and oxytocin helps maintain the more balanced security and connectivity of daily love.

It is unusual to see couples who have been married for over seven years to have pounding hearts and sweaty palms when they see each other on a daily basis. However, this certainly does not mean that love fades over time. Rather, the heightened initial physiological response transitions to a more steady state of love equilibrium. At midlife, when sex steroid hormones are declining, the physiological status of the love equilibrium may shift, especially if regular attention to love "booster shots" is neglected. Too often, if a man feels neglected and seeks a hormonal boost in the form of a midlife extramarital affair, we refer to it as his midlife crisis. In reality, he is seeking outpatient therapy rather than a relationship, but he may destroy his own relationship with his wife in the process. A woman who feels neglected by her husband may grow sullen and depressed as her own bonding hormones become depleted.

A downhill emotional spiral may lead to withdrawal of love and affection. That is why the secrets of romance can unleash the hormones of passion . . . especially at midlife. And the best news is that we can activate our own romantic hormones. Our neural circuits have an incredible neuromemory of stored romantic feelings and physiological states. We can recapture and stimulate our love hormones with a bit of knowledge, a true desire, and a real commitment to our relationship.

Twenty Fun Ways to Activate Your Romance Hormones, *and* Keep Your Lover

1. Let memories linger. When was the last time that you sat down with your partner and took a stroll down memory lane? Thinking about how and when you met, your first date, your first romantic encounter, or your first kiss, can stimulate not only your thoughts but your hormonal memories as well. Reviving the feelings that accompanied these memories can actually reinvigorate neural and hormonal processes. Tapping into past hormonal surges can stimulate and rekindle current emotions as well.

2. Revive honeymoon nostalgia. Some couples report that visiting their old honeymoon suite at the hotel they stayed in after the wedding stirs up those passionate juices. Visiting old romantic haunts, listening to music from your courtship days, and watching old movies can revive those old loving feelings. The molecules of emotion go into action when they are revived.

3. As a love-work assignment, write each other a list on one of the following topics:
   10 Reasons Why I Love You
   10 Reasons Why I Married You
   10 Reasons Why I Want to Spend the Rest of My Life with You
Exchange lists over a candlelit dinner for two, only one list per dinner. Do this for three weeks in a row, then make a candlelit dinner for two a weekly event, even without the list exchange.

4. Use the power of touch. Take turns giving each other nonsexual massages. The sheer act of touching each other's skin will release oxytocin hormone and enhance your feelings of closeness. Intimacy goes beyond sexuality. Couples who remain close emotionally make a habit of touching each other. It's as if there is a synergy of soul that is recharged each time we come into physical contact with our loving partner. Couples who go to bed at the same time, even in the absence

of intercourse, will have greater intimacy than those who are on different sleep cycles.

Couples who avoid physical intimacy also suffer from emotional isolation and have greater rates of depression, irritability, disease, and divorce.

Massage has also been shown to enhance immunity. Even in the clinical setting, the gentle touch of a physician can strengthen the healing process. The gentle touch of a loving partner can certainly enhance passion and intimacy.

5. Use the the power of scent. Certain aromas can elicit specific physiological responses as well as romantic memories. Human pheromones enhance sensuality and/or sexuality. Consciously, or unconsciously, certain aromas register at higher cortical (brain center) levels that stimulate physical and emotional responses. Aromatherapy can be used to create a more intimate and relaxing environment. Discover which scents stir the right feelings for you and your partner.

Specific fragrances and perfumes in women, or after-shave lotions in men, may have similar effects on the opposite sex. In the movie *The Scent of a Woman,* Al Pacino, a blind man, compensates for his lack of sight by enjoying the sensuality of a woman through his senses of smell and touch.

6. Read romance novels together. In *The Bridges of Madison County,* author Robert James Waller created a midlife romance so alive and real that readers called the *National Geographic* magazine hoping to learn more about the fictional character Robert Kincaid, a 52-year-old divorced photographer. In this memorable tale of midlife love, passions flourish with such authenticity that the renewed hormonal response in the fictional characters transcends the written word. As one reviewer from barnesandnoble.com commented, "Keep this book in mind if you ever feel the love slipping from your life. I guarantee a newly found passion after reading this book."

While *The Bridges of Madison County* explores midlife passion from an extramarital perspective, one that cannot be advocated, Nicholas Sparks's *The Notebook* models married lifelong soul mates sharing their real passions and everlasting love into eternity. Sparks shows that romance and passion are possible at any age and the purity and intensity of the love deepens within the sanctity of midlife marriage. Both novels are recommended reading for passion awareness.

7. Share your romantic thoughts. Skim through magazines and books to discover what you and your partner consider sexy and stimulating. Guys, read her romance novels and find out what she finds sexy. Gals, look at some of his favorite magazines and find out what he finds most stimulating. Make a wish list for each other with your top choices of where to go and what to do on your ultimate date.

8. Let pleasant surprises enhance hormonal responsiveness. Have an impromptu celebration about some aspect of your relationship or your partner. Turn it into a special event by going out to celebrate. The event will leave a lasting positive memory both emotionally and physiologically.

9. Pretend you're dating again. Forget that you've been married for 20-something years. Prepare for an evening out together as if it were one of your first dates. Make an extra-special effort to look good for your partner and to be on your best, must-impress behavior.

Guys in particular, watch out for actions of familiarity—that is, less-than-polished behavior such as nose picking or unrestrained bodily sounds (burping, belching, etc.). Be gentlemanly, pull out her chair, open the door, and offer to help her with her coat. Compliment her on her appearance, and yes, tell her how much you appreciate and love her.

Gals, let him know how much you appreciate his taking you out, what a nice evening you had, how you would enjoy going out together again. Don't discuss mundane or domestic problems while on your date together. Don't discuss the bills, kids, or laundry. Don't nag about anything. Show him that you enjoy and appreciate his company. Be in the moment. Let him know he's your special guy.

10. Boost your love hormones. Write your honey a little love note, put it in an envelope with a small piece of chocolate, and place it on your mate's pillow. Irresistible and delicious!

11. Listen to music that puts you both in the mood. Music can bring out emotional responses. Listening to soothing, relaxing music together can harmonize and synchronize your love hormones. Music therapy has been shown to directly affect the mood center of the brain.

12. Read bedtime stories to each other. Reading passages to each other from a favorite book or selections of poetry as a bedtime ritual soothes the soul and is a relaxing treat. When was the last time anyone read you a bedtime story?

13. Leave a surprise love note in an unlikely spot. Repeat often, but not on a regularly scheduled basis. Keep your partner guessing.

14. Give each other a bedtime foot massage. You will want to make this a nightly routine.

15. Surprise your partner with flowers for no special occasion but to show your affection.

16. Create a new ritual together that the two of you will look forward to and enjoy together. For example, take a walk after dinner every Monday, Wednesday, and Friday. Light the fireplace every Tuesday and Thursday evening. Sit down together on the patio before dinner and enjoy a glass of wine.

17. Look at pictures from the early days of your marriage. Talk about what you remember from those times—fond memories only.

18. Give each other a shampoo and scalp massage. Be careful—this one can be addicting. You will want to make this at least a once-a-week routine.

19. Send your partner a written thank-you note for something you really appreciate. Feeling appreciated boosts feelings of self-

satisfaction and raises the brain's neurotransmitter serotonin levels (similar to the effect of some antidepressants). Seeing a thank-you in writing gives extra emphasis and makes it more memorable.

20. Plan a second honeymoon and then make it happen. Enjoy the planning and anticipation. Perhaps it will coincide with an anniversary or a birthday, or invent a completely new date for a second honeymoon romance. Then celebrate the second honeymoon on an annual basis as well.

What to Do When Reality Hits

The week I am writing this offers a sneak preview into my future, as my husband and I will be sampling a taste of empty-nest syndrome. For ten days we will be getting a glimpse of what our real world will be like in a few short years. Our youngest, 11-year-old Lizzy, will be going off for one and a half weeks of adventure at sleepaway camp, while our eldest, 21-year-old Danielle, will be moving to the East Coast to begin medical school. Our middle child, 20-year-old Jeremy, is away at college—far enough away to live outside the home, but close enough to come home for a weekend when the mood strikes or the laundry basket overflows. This will be the first instance in over two decades of inhabiting the family abode without the company of kids. This is quite different from going off on some vacation or work-related trip and hiring a sitter to stay with the kids. We are the ones staying behind (with the pets) and it is the kids who are leaving us. No one has been hired to stay and keep us company.

The challenge is at once exciting, anticipatory, and admittedly, a touch scary. What's a midlife couple to do? Time for rediscovery? Yes. Time to fill the empty nest with a full-spectrum relationship? Yes. Time for romance? Yes, yes. More time for each other equals more time for relationship-enhancing activities such as those outlined earlier in this chapter. Time to fill the void that many, if not all, midlifers encounter at some point in their life journey together.

Romances do flourish when we take the time to recapture the awesomeness in one another.

Balancing time, space, and place becomes critical. Without kids in the immediate foreground, there is opportunity to expand one's horizons and consider charitable options that never before seemed possible. We could both dedicate some of our extra free time to community activities and feel that we are giving something back to society. Staying active physically and professionally is equally important to both of us. Having the luxury of extra time allows us to pursue these goals and add some hobbies that have been put on the back burner.

Some couples look forward to fewer responsibilities while others are anticipating new and varied challenges. Couples who prefer to travel will have the luxury to do so. Others who prefer to be homebodies will also have the luxury to do so. Whatever you may prefer, some form of lifestyle change will occur and it should be anticipated. There is no one right way of doing midlife perfectly, although there are definite pitfalls to be aware of.

Midlife relationships do become vulnerable, but there are strategies that enable couples to become even stronger together. Options of what to do when the going gets rough are explored in the next chapter.

CHAPTER 10

Be Prepared If Turbulence Strikes

Love is an alchemical process in which we are the material to be transmuted.

Thomas Moore, Soul Mates

Midlife is a time of challenge for both men and women. Understanding the changes and challenges that accompany your partner's transition is the first step to a smooth journey. Having the right balance of love, friendship, respect, intimacy, and spirituality is a goal for all couples. At midlife this balance is frequently tested by changing life circumstances, hormonal shifts, physical changes, and emotional fluctuations. Multiply these effects by not one, but two members of a midlife partnership and the impact grows exponentially. It may seem ironic, but there is some comfort in knowing that challenges are a normal and healthy necessity for the growth of a relationship. The old adage "No pain, no gain" has been replaced with "No challenge, no change."

Please Keep Your Seat Belts Fastened

Recently I was on a cross-country flight to the East Coast when the all too familiar overhead warning light came on: FASTEN SEAT BELTS PLEASE. There had been no prior announcement from the pilot as the flight attendants scurried up and down the aisles checking for passenger compliance. I was somewhere between half dozing and half reading when the sudden shaking of the plane jolted me into crisp alertness. I am a frequent enough flier to understand that turbulence does occur, but something was different this time. The rocking and rolling of the plane persisted for at least 45 minutes. I was becoming increasingly uncomfortable. *Why am I getting so anxious? I've been through this kind of thing before,* I wondered to myself.

My heart rate seemed to be approaching my aerobic target zone and yet I was sitting still. Finally, the plane settled into smoother air, the Fasten Seat Belts sign went off, and I could start to analyze my own reaction. I realized what had been different this time: I had been waiting (consciously and/or subconsciously) for an explanation. Not hearing from the pilot that he was aware and was taking steps to do something left me feeling somewhat helpless and more anxious. Now my rational mind knew that the pilot obviously was aware and knew how to handle the situation, but the lack of communication to the passengers left this particular passenger in a high anxiety state.

On the return trip to the West Coast, we again encountered turbulence, but this time there was some commentary from the pilot. "Folks, we're going to experience some choppiness up here shortly, so I'm going to ask you all to put your seat belts back on. We'll be climbing to a higher altitude to find smoother air." The turbulence was no better or worse than that experienced previously. However, my reaction was completely different. This time, I felt quite calm— my rational mind was in harmony with my subconscious. I no longer had a physiological response to the turbulence (no rapid heartbeat) and I felt greater confidence in the pilot.

Clearly the difference between these two incidents of turbulence was the communication from the pilot. Pilot number one did not acknowledge the turbulence to the passengers. Pilot number two communicated directly with the passengers, acknowledging the conditions and what attempts he would be making to improve the situation. It was not so much the turbulence that created the anxiety for me as it was the lack of communication from the person in charge.

Just as it is unrealistic to expect a long-haul flight to be turbulence free, so too is it impractical to anticipate a long-term relationship to be trouble free. The key to preventing undue anxiety and loss of confidence in each party is to keep the lines of communication flowing freely. If one partner is having a rough time and can't or won't communicate with the other partner, both parties become distressed and the relationship takes on anxiety. We may have to buckle up during trying times, but we shouldn't feel the need to kick open the emergency exit door during a bout of turbulence. Too often, especially during midlife, the essence of communication seems to dwindle and the impulse to make an emergency departure starts to make headway. I recommend that every couple anticipate turbulence, look for it, talk about it, and stay buckled up. Work for and seek out the smoother ride ahead. Choppiness is not an end in itself but a means to achieving a better result.

Four Surefire Ways to Wreck a Long-Term Relationship

Faultfinding

"If only he would stop being so critical. It seems as if we can hardly have a normal conversation these days without one of us jumping in to criticize the other. Sometimes it escalates to the point where I feel we're each trying to outdo the other in criticism. It's a 'Can you top this?' contest. We are definitely in a downward spiral and neither of us is winning." Fifty-two-year-old Hannah vented her frustration about Richard, her husband of 33 years. She readily admitted that she was an active participant in the contest, but felt that Richard was usually the one to initiate the criticisms. I suggested to Hannah that we look more closely at what was actually happening here, and that she try to be as objective as possible—even trying to see certain situations through Richard's eyes.

Hannah confided that Richard, who recently turned 55, was

having a hard time accepting the fact that he was starting to slow down physically. I asked Hannah what she meant by Richard slowing down. "Well, I'll give you an example," she replied. "Richard used to be an avid jogger, trying to run at least three miles a day, five or six times a week. Last year his knees started to bother him and his doctor said he would need knee surgery if he continued that amount of running. So he cut it out altogether and, as far as I can tell, he really hasn't substituted any other form of physical activity. So it's not surprising that he has put on about twenty pounds because he didn't cut back on his eating. If anything, he seems to be less concerned about his food choices and keeps on putting on the weight. I know he must hate that mini-pregnancy that he's carrying around with him all the time now. But nothing I seem to do or say makes a difference. It's so frustrating because he used to care about taking care of himself. Now it seems as if all he cares about is picking on me."

I told Hannah how hard it is to see the tornado, especially since she was in the middle of the storm. But I shared with her that it seemed that Richard was indeed critical and this was a symptom of his own inability to deal with his own problems. Rather than tackle his weight issue or his lack of motivation to find a new form of exercise, he projected his displeasure with himself and vented his anger on Hannah. Often it is the nearest and the dearest who bears the burden of projected self-criticism. I reassured Hannah that this was more about Richard than it was about her. However, she was feeding into the criticism frenzy by becoming an active and willing participant. Rather than break the vicious downward spiral, she fueled it.

I explained to Hannah that she had two choices. Choice one: She could continue the trend and anticipate a crash landing. Statistics show that couples who are constantly critical of each other, especially if the man criticizes the woman, have a very high chance of divorcing. This is particularly true at midlife, when there is heightened sensitivity on each side. Choice two: She could break the vicious cycle by choosing to ride the smoother current. I suggested she fly at a higher altitude, thereby elevating herself a safe measure above the turbulence. "Well, how do I do that?" was her logical question.

I recommended that she listen but not respond back with any criticism whatsoever. If there was any validity to Richard's criticism, she might even acknowledge it and offer to make some changes. If she felt there was no merit to Richard's faultfinding, then she was to acknowledge to herself that this was Richard's way of dealing with his own self-displeasure. By not criticizing back, she would disarm him. To help him find a better way, she should be prepared to offer positive solutions. For example, since Hannah was upset (and presumably Richard was, too) with his weight gain and lack of exercise, she could initiate walks together. That way Richard wouldn't be stressing his knees with the hard pounding of running and they both would have a new mode of communication. She could also stop picking on Richard's poor food choices and focus on bringing home only healthful foods.

If Richard didn't respond to her positive overtures and her ceasefire in the arena of criticism, she might suggest he seek professional help. Men in midlife who are perpetually critical, irritable, or angry have a higher chance of being depressed. Since Richard was upset about slowing down (getting older and the physical changes that he was experiencing), depression might be playing a role as well. A thorough physical would be helpful.

Hannah came back to see me three months later. I was happy to hear that she and Richard were both flying together at a higher altitude and the ride was considerably smoother. Their evening walks together were something they both cherished, and Richard was also feeling much better about losing his unwanted fat.

Scorn

While constant criticism is bad, having scorn for your partner is even worse. In fact, if you or your partner are at this stage, the only solution is to check yourselves into couples' intensive care. Nothing ruins unconditional love more than disdain for your partner. And it often takes some time and effort to reach such a stage. Sometimes it happens without your actually realizing how it got there. The foundation for contempt can be built with criticism and loss of respect. Unhealed criticism leaves festering wounds and scars. As these scars coalesce, there is less fresh, clean surface to work with. Assuming an initial foundation based on love, the surface now becomes so defaced with the scars of criticism and fighting that it is almost impossible to recognize the earlier, sweeter layers of caring, kindness, and cooperation. However, they are still there, buried beneath the surface, and can be retrieved with the right motivation, effort, and skills.

Long-term relationships sometimes develop layers over the years and may reach critical mass when there is too much layering of old baggage. That is when scorn sets in. Add some elements of personal vulnerability, self-doubt, and hormonal shifts, and spontaneous combustion might occur. Peel back the layers. Get back down to the friendship level.

Sometimes this is easier said than done. If there is a true desire to reinstate love and exorcise contempt, you and your partner have to pull together. By revisiting the happier times in the relationship, you are able to tap into stored feelings of mutual love and understanding. If you nurture these past memories with current acts of kindness, a new awareness will unfold. Developing a heightened sensitivity to each others' needs at this stage of life will open the path to intimacy once again.

Withdrawal

Gloria feels that Keith is not himself lately. Although he doesn't complain, he acts as if he has lost a close buddy—his thoughts drift, his brow is furrowed, his entire being is preoccupied with worrisome thoughts. Lately his sleep is fitful and his snoring is unbearable.

Fifty-five-year-old Keith knows Gloria is not the same woman he married over 25 years ago. She was always so carefree in her 20s. Lately, everything pushes her into a rage. Although Keith tries to tread lightly, Gloria seems to erupt without reason.

As far as sex—that used to be fun, but now Gloria and Keith never seem to be in the right mood together at the same time. Keith wonders if their libidos are out of sync. Gloria secretly fears her libido is out of existence. What with the change in her moods, her fuzzy-headedness, and roller-coaster emotions, Gloria knows something is not right. Why, she wonders silently, can't she concentrate or remember things or juggle life the way she used to? Keith wonders to himself what life is turning into. *What is happening to me? What is becoming of her?* Too often, midlife partners retreat quietly into their own lonely corners to suffer in silence and wonder what the other might be thinking. Rather than open up and reach out, they put up an emotional wall.

Men are more prone to withdrawal than women; however, women are not completely immune. A man may secretly and anxiously wonder about the types of physical and emotional changes he is experiencing. Not realizing that close to 70 percent of the male population in his age bracket is experiencing similar symptoms, he is afraid of abandoning the macho image and exposing his authentic self—even to his spouse. So instead he withdraws. The more she might try to get him to open up, the more he retreats. While he struggles silently, she suffers as well. Continually withdrawing can lead to resentment, emotional distancing, and even depression.

Learning to turn toward each other again rather than away can help break the withdrawal mode. If you recognize yourself or your partner in this mode, start by taking baby steps in the right direction. You might be the first to confide your inner thoughts to the other. Share them openly with your mate and see what impact they have. Let your mate know that you are genuinely interested in what he or she is experiencing and show your empathy. Affectionately acknowledging that his change of life can be as challenging as hers validates his inner concerns and gives him a sense of relief that he is not alone.

Many macho men feel an intense sense of relief knowing that their mate is on their side offering support and love through a difficult time. By reconnecting with each other rather than withdrawing, the midlife couple make their relationship an even safer harbor. She doesn't have to find emotional fulfillment outside of the relationship, while he is reassured that his feelings and needs are understood.

Loss of Trust

By definition, trust is the firm belief in the honesty and reliability of another; it is the confident expectation and responsibility resulting from faith placed in another. Indeed, trust is the lifeblood of every healthy, successful midlife relationship. Without trust, there is no sense of immunity from the pressures and evils of the outside world. In particular, trust becomes an almost sacred commodity at midlife. This is a time of transition for both the man and the woman. Sometimes couples are surrounded by self-doubt, a form of distrust of self. There are so many changes occurring on both the physical and the emotional levels. This is a critical time when trust in one another becomes a vital anchor, especially in a rocky sea.

If trust dissolves, the relationship may follow suit. That is why it is critical to reinforce and restore trust immediately if there is any erosion.

The Cyberaffair

Toby, a stunning 45-year-old redhead, has been my patient for over 10 years. She is typically a delight to take care of. Always in an upbeat mood, she maintains an active lifestyle and is conscientious about her health. I will never forget her last appointment with me.

My nurse came in to forewarn me. "Dr. Cetel, Toby is here and I can't get her to stop crying." By the time I entered the exam room, Toby's eyes were beet red and she had already emptied half of the tissue box. I sensed her despair instantly.

"Toby." I put my arms around her. Adrenaline was rushing through my system and my thoughts were going wild. Did she lose a loved one? Did a parent or best friend die? What could be going on to cause such a reaction. And then she told me.

"Chuck has been confiding in another woman," she wailed. "Every night he sits at that darn computer, supposedly working on business projects. More often than not, I wind up going to bed alone because he's still 'working' at the computer. Yesterday, I went into the office after he thought I was sleeping. He went to the kitchen to take a break and I could see the message he was sending to this other woman. When he came back, I confronted him with it. He laughed and said it was harmless because she lived in Australia and there could never be any physical contact. That made me even more furious. Does he think I'm an idiot? Carrying on all that time, having me think he's working when he's having a confidential relationship with another woman. It doesn't matter to me that she lives halfway around the world. It's his dishonesty that I can't fathom.

"Obviously, he was doing this behind my back and didn't want me to know. Now I can't trust him at all, with anything. He says I'm overreacting but I feel as if he stabbed me in the back with his deceit. Doc, I want you to check me out for every sexually transmitted disease known to mankind. Chuck joked that the only thing he could have caught from her was a computer virus, but now that I don't trust him I can't take anything for granted. My marriage is ruined."

I completed Toby's exam, including a thorough check for sexually transmitted diseases. While none was found, it was clear that her husband had so violated her trust that the damage was irreparable. One month later she called to let me know that she was divorcing her husband and moving out of town. She added that she was giving him full custody of the computer.

The moral of the story: Never underestimate the value of trust in a midlife relationship. Once its sanctity is broken, it may be exceedingly difficult to restore. When the infamous Clinton-Lewinsky affair broke, the words "I did not have sex with that woman" came back to destroy not only the trust of a wife and a daughter, but that of an entire nation. Preservation of trust takes precedence over reparation at all times.

Tips for Building a Healthy Midlife Relationship

1. Do unto your partner as you would have your partner do unto you. Create a user-friendly environment. By being the kind of partner that you would want to have for yourself—compassionate, caring, approachable, easy to talk to, willing, and wanting to be listened to—you set the standard for what you expect in return. Bear in mind that a midlife partnership is about give and take, not tit for tat. The benefit of maturity allows you to excel in this arena.

2. What are the three most essential ingredients for a healthy, dynamic, and growing midlife relationship? If you answered communication, communication, and communication, go to the head of the class. When the channels of communication become blurred on a regular basis, couples cannot sustain the essence of the relationship. Poor communication translates into a poor relationship. Develop communication skills such as scheduling regularly appointed "just you and me" get-together times. The simple act of setting aside at least 15 minutes daily just to be in each other's presence, alone and free from the clutter of the outside world, can do wonders to enhance communication. When I hear couples complain that they can't find the time, I give them an ultimatum to make the time. Learn to prioritize sacred couple time.

3. Accept the ups and downs that occur in all long-term relationships. Don't panic when turbulence strikes. Embrace it as a rite of passage—a passage into an even deeper and closer place.

4. Realize that your partner is experiencing similar midlife changes, including emotional ups and downs, physical changes, as well as hormonal shifts. Your mate may not even be tuned in to his or her own midlife transition. Learn as much as you can about your

partner's change of life and use this knowledge to be a willing and loving supporter.

5. Recognize and gently acknowledge your imperfections rather than dwell on your partner's. Having a better understanding and compassion for yourself will allow you to feel more compassion for your partner.

6. Love means never taking your longtime partner for granted.

7. Realize your partner is not a mind reader. Take responsibility for communicating your feelings, dreams, emotions, and needs.

8. Listen with your heart first, eyes second, and ears third.

9. There can never be a surplus of midlife tenderness and affection.

10. Respect your partner and respect yourself.

11. Take pride of ownership in your body and health. You are the responsible party.

12. Share your feelings with your partner, even when the going gets tough. Sharing will lead to greater intimacy when it is done to promote insight and love.

13. Remove blame from your discussions. The manner and the tone in which you address your partner is critical. Starting sentences with "You are" leads to labeling and sets an atmosphere for blame and defensiveness. Substitute "I" as in "I feel insecure when you don't tell me that you're running late. It makes me feel that I'm not important enough for you to consider my feelings." Your feelings are legitimate and offer your partner an insight into your inner self. Rather than search for faults, you are turning to your partner for understanding. This type of discussion promotes empathy in place of blame and defensiveness.

14. Understand and accept that all relationships must be flexible to be strong. Too much rigidity can cause your love boat to rock and capsize rather than sway in the breeze.

15. You and your partner are not the same people you were 20 years ago. Realize that the thread of love, trust, and commitment strengthens the relationship even as you both are facing new challenges.

16. This is not your parents' menopause. You both are blazing new trails together. Consciously and subconsciously, it is hard to deny that you are under the influence of your families of origin. Even though you desire not to repeat your parents' past, there are powerful forces working behind the scenes reinforcing imprinted messages. By recognizing who you are now, and how you want to live the rest of your life together, you will become proactive in designing your destiny.

Take Stock of Your Relationship

Midlife is the ultimate time to take stock of your relationship. You both are in a natural state of reassessment of yourselves, your life's accomplishments, your successes as well as your disappointments. Sometimes your self-assessment may be less than stellar. What areas need upgrading? What needs a bit of remodeling? Only if you permit yourselves the luxury of facing these questions will you be capable of continued growth, not only for yourselves as individuals but for yourselves as a couple. Without growth, there is only stagnation.

It is not unusual for midlife couples to grow tired of what seems like the same old routine. Too often one partner feels neglected or taken for granted while the other partner doesn't have a clue. Up until midlife there is an abundance of distractions to keep the typical couple preoccupied with everything but their relationship. Career obligations, growing kids, and even aging parents consume an enormous amount of energy and time. Then things change. Kids move out, careers simmer down, we get help with our parents, and we are left to face one another. No wonder when we reach the middle stage of our life there is often an awkward void. Rather than tackle the void, too often there is an attempt to flee. And often one partner has no clue what is going on with the other. Neither husband nor wife is happy with the way their lives are going, yet they are unable to communicate their feelings to each other. This is also the time for hormonal changes in both the man and the woman. No wonder marriage satisfaction is low at midlife.

With all these changing variables, it is not surprising that midlife relationships are particularly fragile as reflected in high divorce rates. If the relationship has not been nurtured throughout the years, it will not be self-sustaining. Just as a garden will not survive without ongoing weeding, pruning, watering, and fertilizing, neither will a relationship. Just as a new car cannot go on indefinitely without an oil change or a tune-up, neither can a relationship. We wouldn't think of waiting until our car breaks down on the freeway to take action to fix it. Nor would we abandon a car midtrip that just needed more gas. Then why do so many midlife couples do this with their relationships? A word to the wise: best to intervene before the red warning light comes on. That is why this is the perfect time for couple's time out—the art of rediscovering and reinforcing your love for each other.

Time Out

When was the last time the two of you had a honeymoon? If you answer yes to any of the following: (a) I don't remember, (b) Over 10 years ago, or (c) What is a honeymoon? then you are both definitely overdue for a honeymoon-type experience—with a twist. The twist is to savor the experience from a higher place of maturity and love. This particular honeymoon is more about rediscovering each other as individuals and as a couple in healthy transition. Forty-nine-year-old Karen and 53-year-old Steve were able to move from a place of stress and staleness in their 22-year marriage to a level of deep understanding, commitment, and love for each other. What was their secret?

Meet Me in Hawaii

When Karen told Steve that she was planning a surprise for their anniversary, his main concern was that it did not interfere with the play-offs for the Super Bowl. His negativity and level of enthusiasm were enough to make Karen cry, and secretly she was entertaining thoughts of leaving Steve. She felt so guilty, especially when she looked through the personal ads in the local paper, fantasizing what it might be like with another man—the man of her dreams.

It was frightening how lonely and desperate Karen had become. She felt starved for affection and emotionally out of tune with Steve. And she knew he didn't have a clue. Worse yet, even if he did know, she was sure he wouldn't even care. Karen realized that, if their relationship was to survive, they both needed to make some changes. As far as she could tell, Steve seemed content. He would tell their friends they were happily married. Karen would always cringe when she heard those words.

It was time for a change and Karen knew it would be up to her. She took the bold step of setting up their reservations. When Steve said he couldn't make it for the first day, Karen didn't want to hear why. This was their anniversary week. She decided to keep the reservation and told Steve to meet her in Hawaii.

Karen made the six-hour flight alone. What a way to start an anniversary vacation! Would Steve be joining her? At that point she wasn't sure. What he didn't know was that Karen had signed them up for a one-week Tantra course called "The Art of Conscious Loving." It was primarily for couples, but individuals would be paired with a partner, so no one would be alone. She promised herself not to chicken out if Steve didn't show. Karen was amazed at her own gutsiness.

When Steve arrived at the hotel, he looked like a wounded puppy.

Karen's determination to take this trip had been a wake-up call. He also had a long, lonely six-hour flight to think about their relationship. Steve realized they needed to make some repairs. He greeted Karen with a long and gentle hug. It felt right to be together and he apologized for his stubbornness in coming to Hawaii. They were ready for a new beginning.

Welcome to Tantra

Tantra teaches that lovemaking between a man and a woman, when practiced with focus and awareness, can become a path to both spiritual and sexual ecstasy. The term *Tantra* literally refers to a 2,000-year-old series of Hindu texts that describe sexual disciplines, rituals, and meditations originally written in the form of a dialogue between a male god and his female companion. In India, traditional "Tantrikas" spent years under the guidance of a spiritual teacher who instructed them in yogic rituals that purify the mind and body. Over time, these techniques were meant to energize the pysche into a higher state of consciousness. Only then would the participant be ready to partake in sexual rites with a partner. At that point, through the sacred act of love, the Tantric couple merged their sexuality into an ecstatic union. Ancient Tantra represents a spiritual system where sexual love is considered a sacrament. Tantric sex is about intimate, spontaneous, and meditative lovemaking with your partner.

Charles and Caroline Muir have developed a popular seminar series based on Tantric philosophical concepts. Their course, "The Art of Conscious Loving," aims to open individuals to transformational lovemaking through spiritual awareness. Over the years their course has been quite successful and has helped couples deepen their relationships with intimacy and passion. When Karen's longtime friend and teaching colleague Pauline returned raving about the best thing that could have happened for her marriage, Karen knew she had to hear all about it. If this program had helped revive Pauline's 20-year-plus marriage (one that Pauline had described as stale and cold), then there was hope for her own. There was also some comfort in knowing that other couples in their age group were experiencing similar problems and that they were not alone.

Karen was so taken by the dramatic change in Pauline's attitude and outlook that she quickly overcame her own negative stereotypes that anything to do with yogic philosophy was too far out. Now she and Steve were about to enter the world of Tantric teachings. One of the basic premises of Tantrism is that male and female are viewed as two polarities that meet and merge to create wholeness. In Tantra, the man can explore his softer, more vulnerable and feminine aspects. He can escape from the societal stereotype of male responsibilities and make love without a goal orientation or performance anxiety. Likewise, the woman can explore her masculine side and create new ways of giving and receiving pleasure for both herself and her partner. This does not imply role reversal between the man and the woman but helps expand each partner's sense of masculinity and femininity to include the other's.

For Steve and Karen the one-week workshop in Hawaii provided the tools necessary to relate to each other in a significantly better way. This was not a temporary fix. One year later, their heightened awareness of each other and their enhanced love and passion for each other have become a permanent part of their relationship. By maintaining their practice of the Tantric principles, they have kept their commitment to each other and the relationship. Tantric practitioners are reminded that "nothing is more important than your love, harmony, and connection as a couple." In our modern, hurry-up society, such a philosophy may be lost in the shuffle of day-to-day living. Since conscious lovemaking does not come naturally, Karen had to make a conscious decision to learn and embrace this tradition with Steve. Together they saved their relationship.

A Funny Thing Happened on the Way to the Video Store

It hardly seemed like a funny story, but 53-year-old Cindy was laughing as she told it. Her audience was a room full of sweaty, hard-breathing 40-year-old women who had come to the gym for a morning class of step aerobics. I was among the group, grunting with the best of them. Over the sound of the throbbing beat, Cindy described why she always feels strange about going to a Videos Unlimited Video store. Her chattiness helped make the class seem shorter than it was.

"My husband, Wayne, left ten years ago to return a movie to Videos Unlimited Video and I haven't seen him since. Now every time I go into a Videos Unlimited, I think about Wayne being overdue. It's funny how we have those associations." Cindy didn't miss a beat or a step while telling her story. Apparently 10 years of healing and a new boyfriend had helped ease the pain and shock that she initially felt.

How can a couple who have lived together for over 20 years be so unaware of each other? Is it a bad case of lack of communication, or is something deeper going on? In his book *Soul Mates: Honoring the Mysteries of Love and Relationship,* Thomas Moore writes:

> The problem in such relationships is not simply a lack of communication, but a sense that experience is meaningless. There seems to be a widespread tendency in modern life to observe events as they happen passively, with gauze in front of one's eyes, like Camus's "stranger," whose detached passivity stems from a complete equalization of values. Nothing is shocking, there are no problems, things happen, there is nothing to be done, said, or thought. Yet certain situations cry out for reflection. . . . The person who can't read his partner of several years probably has little idea of the themes buried within his own life and emotions. Conversely, a person attuned to the mysteries of her own soul will know how to respond to her partner's as well.

Cindy's description of her husband leaving to return a movie and never returning himself appeared to come out of thin air. I suspect there were many deeper layers of changing needs, both physical and emotional, on both sides of the relationship. Cindy added with a laugh that she was having a "bad hormone year" at that time, "but he still shouldn't have run away." Perhaps Wayne was having a bad hormone year as well. One can only speculate.

A Higher Level

A relationship is a living entity that requires continual care. As we mature there is even greater need for attention, time, and loving renewal. There are no automatic upgrades. By being tuned in to your own needs, you can reflect upon yourself and realize that your partner may be experiencing similar emotions and thoughts. Turbulence can be your wake-up call that it is time to move on to a higher level. By taking positive steps, you can achieve a higher degree of harmony with your partner.

Thomas Moore eloquently states:

> Caring for the soul in our relationships, and through them, we can enjoy them both practically and mystically, and with genuine guidance for individuality in others, in the relationship itself, and in ourselves. We can let unplanned developments happen, allow people to change, tolerate our own idiosyncratic needs and cravings, and enjoy and appreciate a community of individuals who may think differently than we do, live oddly, and express themselves none too rationally. For this is what relationship is about: the discovery of the multitude of ways soul is incarnated in this world.

Midlife is not only the epicenter of hormonal change but the launchpad for unprecedented emotional and spiritual growth. It is the time of life to combine the harvests of our personal growth with our partner's and enjoy the feast.

CHAPTER 11

The Truth about Anti-Aging

Nobody grows old by merely living a number of years.
People grow old by deserting their ideals. Years may wrinkle
the skin, but to give up enthusiasm wrinkles the soul.
   Worry, fear, self-distrust bows the heart and turns the
spirit back to dust.

General Douglas MacArthur

At midlife we come to the realization that time is not infinite. Only
what is truly important will take precedence. We know that the time
left for important work or change is running out. Simultaneously,
just as we are becoming more philosophical about the aging process,
our take-charge meno-boomer personalities are avidly following
every new study and every new prediction of an enhanced longevity.
When we read reports that life expectancy in the twenty-first century
is anticipated to be 126 years, we mentally gear up for this possibility. In the meantime, medical and scientific research goes full steam
ahead as we relentlessly lust after any and all anti-aging antidotes.
From endless erections to infinite energy, we want it all. And guess
what? As any spoiled modern baby boomer knows, the future holds
infinite possibilities. After all, this is not our parents' menopause.

An Ageless Society?

From an evolutionary point of view, growing old is a relatively new
phenomenon. In 100 B.C., at the time of Caesar, life expectancy was
only 25 years. By 1900, at the turn of the twentieth century in the

United States, life expectancy had almost doubled, to an average age of 49 years. Menopause was not a big concern, as most women and men did not live long enough to experience this physiological occurrence. In 2000, the average life expectancy is 79.7 years for women and 72.9 years for men. A child born in 1997 can anticipate living to 76.5 years, almost 30 years longer than a child born at the turn of the twentieth century. Today, a man who reaches age 65 can expect to live to 80.5 years, while a woman who turns 54 can anticipate reaching the age of 84.3 years. Currently, the fastest-growing segment of the American population is 85 years and over. By 2010, it is estimated that there will be 160,000 centenarians living in the United States. Between 1998 and 2025, it is expected that the over-65 population will have expanded by 200 percent, with 20 percent of the population in 2030 age 65 or older.

Are we a rapidly aging society? The answer is overwhelmingly yes. As a culture are we interested in promoting healthy longevity and maximizing life expectancy? Again the answer is overwhelmingly yes. As we live longer do we really want to get older? Ironically, the answer is a resounding no. Is it possible to live longer while aging less? Possibly.

Living Younger Longer: The World of Anti-Aging Medicine

Anti-aging medicine represents a paradigm shift from disease-based medicine to prevention and reversal of age-related diseases. As people live longer, practitioners of anti-aging medicine seek to enhance the quality of life, as well as the quantity, by using a variety of technology, treatments, or interventions for early detection, prevention, and reversal of age-related disease. In essence it is an extension of preventive medicine to the ultimate degree with an emphasis on research to prolong and increase the quality of life.

Examples of potential anti-aging strategies include the following:

- Designer hormone therapies
- Stem cell therapies
- Bioengineered organ parts
- Novel systems for the delivery of medications and natural hormones
- Genetically engineered methods for the delivery of artificial human chromosomes

Do You Know What Your Longevity Quotient Is?

LQ stands for longevity quotient. Unlike IQ, LQ measures your current longevity status rather than your intellectual status. LQ is an assessment of how intelligent you are about living your life on a day-to-day basis with the long-term goal of health and longevity. The good news is that *what you do on a day-to-day basis can have a positive impact on LQ. Conversely, your actions, if left unchanged, may have a negative impact on LQ.* Overall, you have a better chance of improving your LQ by making small positive modifications in your lifestyle that are cumulative. Each new day brings another chance to improve your health. So let's get started.

Scoring System

ACTION	ADD	SUBTRACT
Stretching to improve flexibility	1	
Brushing teeth	1	
Flossing teeth	1	
Exercising moderately (> 20 minutes)	2	
Being sedentary		2
Strength training	2	
Smoking (per cigarette or cigar)		1

ACTION	ADD	SUBTRACT
Drinking > 3 alcoholic drinks/day		2
Drinking > 3 caffeinated drinks/day		2
Eating 4–5 servings fruits and vegetables/day	1/serving	
Eating high-fat foods (> 30% fat)		2
Wearing sunblock	1	
Eating high-fiber foods	1/serving	
Eating excessive calories		1/meal
Eating fish	1	
Eating fried foods		1
Taking multivitamins, antioxidant supplements and/or calcium supplements	1	
Driving while feeling angry		2
Driving without seat belt		2
Stressing out		2/event
Relaxation time (meditation, music, quiet time)	1	
Adequate sleep (7–8 hours)	1	
Inadequate sleep (< 6 hours)		1
Having a soul mate	2	
Having close friends	1	
Having a hobby	1	
Having a good belly laugh	1	
No significant other		1
No social support		2
Volunteering–giving of oneself	1	
Being health-minded (reading or listening to health-related information regularly)	1	

Total:

LQ Score: 15–25: Reasonable longevity
Greater than 25*: Enhanced longevity
Less than 15: Longevity modifications needed

20 Ways to Maximize Your Personal Longevity Quotient

1. Reevaluate and redesign your diet. Don't underestimate the importance of what we put into our mouths and the impact on overall health and vitality. Eating a well-balanced, low-fat, low-sodium diet of minimally processed foods provides a healthy anti-aging foundation. Increase your consumption of fresh fruits and vegetables (five to six servings per day) while diminishing the amount of processed foods, which often have higher fat content and minimal nutrients. Reduce overall saturated fat and animal fat intake and avoid processed carbohydrates such as bread, sugar, pasta, bagels, and rice. Eat adequate amounts of essential fatty acids such as those found in fish and fish oils, nuts, and flaxseed oil (in particular, omega-3). Drink at least two quarts of water daily (eight to ten 8-ounce glasses every day). Water serves as a natural appetite suppressor while helping to metabolize fat, eliminate body waste, prevent constipation, and maintain adequate kidney function.

2. Less may be better. It is not only a matter of what you eat, but how much you eat that really counts toward enhancing longevity. According to Dr. Roy Walford, director of the Gerontology Research Laboratory at the UCLA School of Medicine, "You can extend longevity by restricting food even after full adulthood and middle age." Caloric restriction appears to increase life-span by decreasing the rate of aging and delaying the onset of serious disease. In over 70 years of animal experimentation with such mammals as mice, rats, dogs, and monkeys, cutting calories by 30 to 40 percent led to a life expectancy that was one-third to one-half longer than the non-caloric-restricted animals. Why does this occur?

When calories are significantly restricted, a number of age-related and life-shortening processes are inhibited. To begin with, free radical production is reduced. Free radicals are molecules that are produced with defective electrons in their outer shell. Instead of having paired electrons, as is typical in a stable molecule, the free radical molecule has a single electron, causing it to be unstable and resulting in damage to other cell structures. The fewer free radicals, the less potential for cell damage, disease, and accelerated aging. The incidence of diseases of all kinds is reduced as well as the incidence of cancer. Caloric restriction also enhances the immune response by delaying the normal age-related decline in immunity. Blood sugar and insulin levels drop. Higher levels of sugar and insulin are related to several chronic diseases including heart disease, cancer, and possibly brain deterioration.

According to Dr. Walford, to obtain the maximum anti-aging benefits from caloric restriction, one would have to drop his or her weight to 10 to 25 percent below the ideal body weight. The ideal body weight takes into account a person's height, age, sex, and frame. Dropping 30 to 40 percent below normal, as in the animal experiments, would not be tolerated by most people and would be too extreme. However, even cutting calorie intake by just 12 percent below normal delays aging signs and adds time to an animal's life spans, most likely by reducing the production of damaging free radicals. Certainly, going in the opposite direction—adding calories and gaining weight—will promote free radical production, decrease immunity, and accelerate the aging process.

Try to reduce calories gradually by spacing them throughout the day in five mini-meals to prevent hunger and maintain energy levels. There should be enough calorie intake to allow for moderate exercise on a daily basis. For an active healthy male, 2,000 calories per day should be adequate, while 1,800 calories should suffice for a female. Food intake can then be adjusted based on energy requirements and whether the individual is losing too quickly, too slowly, or not at all. A downfall for many midlife couples is the eating-out syndrome. Typically restaurant portions are far too massive while the calorie and fat content in a single restaurant meal can exceed the recommendations for an entire day. Incorporate meal splitting for portion control. Be proactive when placing your order. Ask for sauces, dressings, butter, sour cream, and other high-fat toppings on the side or not at all. Avoid fried foods and opt for baked, broiled, grilled, or poached dishes. These simple changes are easy to accommodate and can result in enormous benefits for the overall quality of your diet. Over time, it can make eating out a less deadly experience.

3. Be willing to make changes. Use fresh fruit and vegetables in generous amounts. If you must use canned fruit, limit choices to those packed in water or light syrup rather than heavy syrup. If fresh vegetables aren't in season, use fresh frozen as an alternative to canned whenever possible.

Opt for low-fat cooking methods whenever possible: broil, grill, poach, bake, steam, and use cooking sprays rather than frying in fats.

Choose skinless chicken or turkey in place of red meats.

4. Feast on fish. By all means, eat at least two or three servings of fish a week. This is an area in my diet where I admit I had to make a very conscious effort to change my old ways. Growing up with fish phobia, I had to gradually introduce seafood into my diet. Now, not only do I tolerate it, I love it. Studies have consistently shown that fish eaters live longer and are not as prone to such aging diseases as heart disease, strokes, diabetes, cancer, and arthritis. In particular, fatty fishes such as salmon, sardines, and tuna have a generous supply of omega-3 fatty acids. These fatty acids are considered "good fat" because they prevent clot formation, protect arteries and joints from inflammation, lower triglyceride levels, raise the good HDL cholesterol levels, and counter the effects of harmful omega-6 fatty acids that promote free radical formation.

It should be noted that the Japanese, who hold the world's record for longevity, consume at least three times more fish than Americans. In a landmark study published in the prestigious medical journal *Lancet,* Dr. M. L. Burr compared the effects of eating at least two servings a week of oily fish while also consuming more fiber or reducing fat in a population of post–heart attack patients. The fish-eating patients had a significant reduction in mortality rates, by about 30 percent.

Fish oil also seems to retard the spread of breast cancer. In an international study of breast cancer death rates in over 30 countries, it was shown that fish-eating populations had significantly lower rates than non–fish eaters. The highest rates were among women who ate animal fats. Looking at Japan again, where women eat the most fish, the death rate from breast cancer is five times lower than in the United States.

For those of you who are vegetarian, you can also get the anti-aging benefits of omega-3 fatty acids in certain plant foods, although they are considered less biologically active than those found in fish. Nuts provide the type of fat that protects heart health and are also a good source of protein. According to the Nurses' Health Study, women who include nuts in their diet five or more times a week are 35 percent less likely to suffer heart attacks than women who rarely eat nuts. Other excellent sources of omega-3 fatty acids include wheat germ oil, walnut oil, canola oil, and flaxseed oil.

5. Soy is great. Another lesson to be learned by examining the Japanese diet is the anti-aging benefits of including soy products in the diet. Until recently, most of us growing up in the United States probably had little exposure to or knowledge of the wonders of the magical soybean. I do believe the soybean is here to stay and will not evaporate as a passing fad. Again, I consciously needed to make modifications to include some form of soy on a daily basis. The overwhelming benefits to longevity and health are what convinced me. Soybeans are storehouses for potent antioxidants and other anti-aging ingredients. They contain a high natural concentration of genisten, an antioxidant that also has anticancer activity. Numerous studies have shown positive effects not only in blocking tumor cell proliferation but also in preventing plaque buildup in arteries.

In a recent study published in the *Journal of Clinical Endocri-*

nology and Metabolism, investigators found that perimenopausal women who for one month consumed a diet containing 36 ounces of soy milk produced less estrogen and progesterone than they produced before adding soy to their diets. The results of the study may have implications for breast cancer prevention by soy dietary intervention.

Men may also be able to cut their risk of prostate cancer by consuming soy products such as one cup of soy milk or one-half cup of tofu daily. Research presented recently at the annual meeting of the American College of Nutrition found that men who ate at least one serving of soy food per day had up to a 70 percent lower risk of prostate cancer than those who did not incorporate soy foods into their diets. An earlier study found similar results for Japanese men who ate tofu. Consider adding his and hers soy shakes to your daily routine.

6. Stay physically active and fit. Exercise at least 20 to 30 minutes a day, most days of the week, with the goal of raising your heartbeat and sweating. Check with a physician before starting any new form of activity. This critical piece of advice may do more to enhance your life expectancy than anything else you may have control over. The ultimate benefits of regular exercise far exceed weight loss or weight maintenance. These benefits are discussed in greater detail shortly.

7. Get rid of the gut. Lower your risk for abdominal obesity syndrome, which has become a major cause of secondary aging in our society. Some people may have a greater genetic predisposition to developing abdominal obesity than others, but it does not occur unless there is a prolonged period of energy excess—that is, stored energy in the form of abdominal fat. Typically, physical inactivity and excessive fat and calorie consumption play a major role. Over time this leads to higher risks for type 2 diabetes as well as heart disease. The good news is that exercise can mobilize the fat reserves from the abdominal region. Studies have shown that even moderate weight

loss from the visceral fat deposits can reduce the diabetes and cardio-vascular risks.

8. Exercise is the ultimate anti-aging elixir. If exercise was available as a once-a-day supplement that offered all of the benefits we typically attribute to exercise (such as weight loss; reduction in the occurrence of heart attack, angina, non-insulin-dependent diabetes, stroke, osteoporosis, and hypertension; enhancement of the immune response; increases in good HDL cholesterol and decreases in bad LDL cholesterol; as well as elevated mood and reduced anxiety, stress, and depression), it would be a blockbuster sellout. No one would ever miss his or her daily dose. Although chronological aging is an inevitable part of living longer, there is scientific evidence that biological aging (the physiology of physical and mental deterioration) can be delayed by a daily dose of exercise.

Different forms of exercise result in different benefits. All of them can improve the quality of life. In general, exercise cuts down mortality rates at any age while improving mental, physical, and emotional capabilities. The good news is that it is seldom too late to start. One doesn't get too old to exercise, one gets too old by not exercising.

9. Get into strength training. Fitness significantly slows degeneration. Both men and women experience a 30 to 40 percent decrease in strength and muscle mass by age 80 years. However, until about age 50, muscle mass is largely maintained but then declines rapidly. A falloff in physical activity adds to age-related decline in strength. However, age-related decline can be successfully overcome with resistance training. Weight training can increase strength by as much as 200 percent. In a group of 85-year-old men and women, just three months of weight training produced increases of between 20 and 40 percent in the amount of weight they could lift and their overall strength capacity. However, the benefits of strength training go far beyond muscle capacity alone. Greater strength helps to prevent hip fractures and osteoporosis, improves circulation, enhances metabo-

lism, and therefore aids in weight reduction and weight maintenance. It also provides greater joint stability, improves bowel and bladder control, enhances self-image, and promotes emotional well-being.

Researchers at the Washington University School of Medicine in St. Louis, Missouri, recently looked at more than 1,700 elderly adults who took part in exercise interventions at four different locations throughout the United States. All the participants were considered frail and at risk for fall-related injuries. The investigators found that even in this more fragile elderly population, not only was physical well-being enhanced, but, overall, participants reported improved emotional health following the exercise intervention.

10. Start an aerobic training program. Hippocrates summed it up well: "That which is used develops, and that which is not used wastes away." If you are feeling run-down, tired, and melancholy and there doesn't appear to be an identifiable cause ("old age" is not an acceptable excuse), the problem may be energy deficiency syndrome. It takes energy to make energy and starting an aerobic exercise program is an ideal way to regenerate and harvest your own energy. Always start with a comprehensive physical from your physician before embarking on a new exercise routine. Our cardiovascular system—indeed, our life force—depends on our ability to transport oxygen (VO_2 capacity) from our lungs, carry it through our circulatory system, and deliver it throughout our body to our vital organs. Without that capability, we cannot live. As this system degenerates over time, we are left feeling worn out, fatigued, old, and even depressed. The good news is that aerobic exercise and endurance training can enhance our VO_2 capacity even into early old age.

In a study of nine elderly men and women (average age 65 years) who had been sedentary for many years, a program of endurance training increased their VO_2 capacity by 20 to 25 percent. VO_2 normally declines by 9 to 10 percent per decade. After the first two months of the program, the participants averaged 41 minutes of exercise per day, four days per week, at an intensity of 80 percent of their maximal heart rate. The exercise program consisted of walking, jogging, or cycling. This was an excellent outcome for this group of former couch potatoes and attests to the resiliency of the human body to respond to physical challenge. It has been shown that highly trained individuals in their 60s can outperform untrained individuals in their 20s. Talk about an antidote to midlife slump!

11. Flex for flexibility. Loss of flexibility is a sign of aging. The adage "Use it or lose it" definitely applies to flexibility over the years. Maintaining some degree of elasticity is critical to the range of motion around the joints and the suppleness of the muscles and connective tissues. Without flexibility, low back pain and weakness become more common with age and can lead to stiffness and immobility. Make sure to include some form of stretching in your daily exercise routine to encourage flexibility. Yoga, t'ai chi, and chi gung are also excellent techniques for enhancing flexibility as well as improving balance.

12. Build your balance. Balance has only recently taken its well-deserved position on the list of must-haves for optimum fitness and should be addressed in your training program. Too often we realize that poor balance plays a part in stumbles or falls that might have been prevented. Unfortunately, broken hips and head trauma account for significant morbidity and mortality in the older population and are the result of poor balance. Even though Katharine Graham was in her 80s and still sharp as a tack, it was a stumble on the sidewalk that led to her demise. Balance, like flexibility, diminishes with age unless we consciously work to improve it. Balance can be regained by focusing part of the exercise routine on the coordination between the brain, the eyes, the inner ear, and the musculoskeletal system.

The efficiency of this brilliant system of proprioceptors, or sensory receptors that keep us informed of our body's position and location in space on a moment-to-moment basis, can improve with practice. Even such simple techniques as walking with one foot in front of the other in a straight line and then reversing, can fine-tune our balance receptors. Standing on one leg at a time and then shifting to the other leg can be practiced even while we brush our teeth in the morning. The benefits do add up over time, and we can regain balance skills that we might not have realized we lost. Too often we become painfully aware of poor balance after a fall.

13. Does more sex equal a longer life? There has been frequent speculation that a happy sex life can lead to a longer life expectancy. Recently, British researchers have shown that sexual activity may have a protective effect on men's health. A study of the behavior and health of 1,000 British men showed that the higher the frequency of orgasm, the lower the mortality risk from coronary heart disease. Death from other causes showed a similar but lower association with frequency of orgasm. Unfortunately, comparable results for women were not available. Perhaps an updated healthy-living campaign should encourage plentiful fresh fruits, vegetables, and orgasms on an equal basis.

14. Exercise your mind. Keep your brain energized and active. Continue to challenge yourself by learning new skills. Just as the muscles in the biceps will atrophy if they are not challenged with resistance training on a regular basis, the brain tissue will also wither if it is not stimulated. Mental challenges are the best form of keeping the brain in optimum condition. Learn new skills and keep the brain juices flowing. At the young age of 83, my mother recently decided to take up bridge. There is no question that she is reaping multiple benefits by challenging herself, learning a new form of card communication, and having fun at the same time. She looks forward to her next lessons and has a sense of enthusiasm that is at once delightful and age defying.

15. Be creative. It's never too late to develop our creative potential. What if Grandma Moses had decided she was too old to try painting in her 70s? Born Anna Mary Robertson, she started painting in her late 70s and continued beyond her one hundredth birthday. In 1960, at age 99, she was commissioned by Random House to

illustrate Clement Moore's famous poem "The Night Before Christmas" and continued to paint 25 more pictures after her one hundredth birthday. She said: "I look back on my life like a good day's work, it was done and I feel satisfied with it. I was happy and contented. I knew nothing better and made the best out of what life offered and life is what we make it, always has been, always will be." One can only speculate if her late-in-life newfound creativity contributed to her longevity and her desire to live and be productive.

There is no doubt that a creative mind keeps you sharper and more aware of life in general. It is a fallacy to believe that if you haven't created your great work by age 45 then there is little hope. On the contrary, we become freer to enjoy and nurture our creative side when the shackles of day-to-day work routines are released and our creative juices are no longer repressed. Tap into that creativity— it just might be the juice flowing from the fountain of youth.

16. Tickle your funny bone. Tap into humor. Science has proven that laughter is not only good medicine but can enhance life. Critical components of our immune system become activated by exposure to humor. At the opposite end of the spectrum, sadness and depression suppress critical immunological factors and diminish life expectancy. Surround yourself with positive-thinking and light-hearted folks. Fortunately, laughter and humor can be wonderfully infectious agents. These agents can have positive and potent effects on mental outlook, energy, and overall positive physiological healing responses.

The release of mood-enhancing endorphins when we laugh triggers a positive physiological response that can nullify more harmful stress-induced hormones. Spend time with funny people and savor the art of sharing jokes so that you give laughter to others. Save your favorite comic strips and bring them out to remind you that humor is always within reach. Laughter is potent medicine, so make a conscious effort to find something to laugh at or someone to laugh with at least once a day. Beware—humor fixes can become happily habit-forming.

17. Stay connected. Being actively connected with family and friends is a vital part of successful aging for anyone who wants to have a productive, happy, healthy, and long life. Being alone and out of touch is life diminishing. Join a group that you have common interests with. Meet new people and encourage new friendships. There is synergy among friends and just being in a supportive environment. Being part of a community on a daily basis makes us feel alive.

18. Allow no time for boredom or negativity. Jonathan Swift wrote, "May you live all the days of your life." When our days become empty, when we feel bored, we lose precious quality living. Our senses, our minds, and our bodies are not stimulated. Boredom is a wake-up call to do something new and intriguing. Taking up a new hobby, finding a new path to walk on, and looking forward to a future event are all antiboredom strategies. Watch out for the negativity factor. Nothing ages the soul like negativity and being surrounded by negative people. Be aware of your own negative thoughts and the amount of time you spend with people who tend to complain excessively. Negativity sucks energy from the heart and the mind. The combination of boredom and negativity can be devastating. To stay young at heart, surround yourself with upbeat and playful people. Choose to make happy events happen and they will. Happy souls send out positive energy. Be a beacon of happiness.

19. Reduce stress, enhance immunity. Learning to relax can add years to your life while chronic stress accelerates the aging process and diminishes immunity. Neuroscientists have shown that people who chronically overreact to stress lead shorter lives and are more susceptible to brain and nervous system disease. This is the result of the body being on physiological overdrive for prolonged periods of time and exposed to higher levels of damaging stress hormones released by the brain and the adrenal glands. Over time, certain disease

states such as hypertension, heart attack, ulcers, migraine headache, irritable bowel syndrome, and reduced immunity can develop as a consequence of the stress response. The antidote is conscious aware-ness and stress reduction exercises. Allow yourself a second chance at childlike playfulness. By letting go of stressful situations that are out of our control, by forgiving and letting go of anger, and by being more open to friendship, we can reduce the level of toxic stress on a day-to-day basis and reap long-term benefits.

20. Consider meditation. Meditation can help you cope with anxiety, reduce stress, and diminish stress-related illness. Scientific studies have shown the physiological effects of meditation on reduc-ing blood pressure, heart rate, and breathing rate. As a result, people who meditate regularly are able to accomplish an on-command re-laxation response. As with other relaxation techniques, meditation can be learned. Practice by setting aside 10 minutes of quiet time each day. Clear your mind of the inside chatter and any thoughts that come by to clutter your head. This may not be easy at first. Close your eyes and become aware of your breathing. Focus on your breathing by taking slow deep breaths, and visualize inhaling posi-tive energy and exhaling negative emotions. Over time this will be-come easier and you will be able to block out distractions while bringing an inner sense of calm on command. This is a wonderful physiological skill worth developing.

Anti-Aging Superhormones

Few scientific findings have generated as much public interest as those of Dr. Daniel Rudman's 1990 landmark study of a small group of elderly men treated with human growth hormone (GH) injections for six months. In that report, GH increased lean body and bone mass, decreased adiposity (central obesity), significantly enhanced sexual function, and restored skin thickness to that of a 50-year-old man. Study participants raved on national television about improved mood, enhanced energy levels, restored libido, newfound muscle mass, and lost wrinkles, attributing all improvements to GH. This scientific legitimization of GH as a form of anti-aging therapy has stimulated tremendous enthusiasm in the public sector and continued interest in the medical community. The promise of perpetual energy, heightened sex drive, firm muscles, and a lean physique has driven interest in growth hormone into a growth industry. Where there is smoke, there's fire; where there is hype, watch for deception.

Understanding the Pros and Cons of Growth Hormone Therapy

Until recently, the use of GH therapy was available only for children with short stature and insufficient growth hormone secretion. For these children, growth hormone replacement would increase their growth velocity and ultimate height. It was often a therapy saved for children who were headed toward dwarfism. Growth hormone is a protein hormone secreted in the anterior pituitary gland in intermittent bursts known as pulsatile release. In children and young adults, the number of bursts ranges from 6 to 11 per day, with most occurring during the sleep cycle. When our mothers told us to go to bed on time and to get enough sleep or we wouldn't grow up nice and tall, they were referring to growth hormone. Growth hormone secretion is also augmented by growth hormone–releasing hormone (GHRH), exercise, sex steroids, and acute use of glucocorticoid steroids. Factors that inhibit GH secretion include obesity, high blood sugar, aging, and chronic glucocorticoid steroid use.

In 1996, the United States Food and Drug Administration approved the use of GH in growth hormone–deficient adults for the first time. This was a breakthrough for the goals of anti-aging medicine. How common is adult growth hormone deficiency? In humans, the amount of growth hormone secretion after age 31 falls by about 25 percent per decade and, in many cases, ultimately stops. At least 50 percent of persons over age 65 may be considered biochemically growth hormone deficient. Growth hormone function is considered critical for healing and tissue repair, brain function, physical health, mental health, muscle growth, bone strength, energy, and overall metabolism.

The growth hormone deficiency of normal aging is also associated with a decrease in the percentage of lean body mass and an increase in that of fat. Statistical analysis has shown a strong correlation between increased adiposity, especially intra-abdominal fat, with decreased frequency of growth hormone secretory episodes. When scientists in London, England, studied the effects of growth hormone or placebo for six months in 24 patients with adult-onset growth hormone deficiency, lean body mass increased by more than 10 percent in the treated group while there was a concomitant 7 percent decrease in adipose tissue volume, mainly at abdominal fat deposits. Decreased bone mineral density is also observed in many adults with GH deficiency. Most of the available studies report increases in bone mineral density with GH therapy. There is also some preliminary evidence that GH may be potentially beneficial as a regulator of cardiac muscle function.

Recently, a group of Italian doctors evaluated a small group of patients with damaged heart tissue and moderate to severe heart failure. GH was given in low doses to patients while their standard heart failure therapy was continued throughout the study. The investigators found that the treatment significantly enhanced the cardiac output and overall efficiency of cardiac energy performance. While these initial studies are encouraging, it should be noted that the study was short term and done on a small trial basis.

With all of these encouraging results, why wouldn't everyone want to be on GH therapy? Perhaps the strongest case for growth hormone replacement therapy is to restore body composition, reduce obesity, particularly around the abdominal region, and increase lean muscle mass. This is an impressive example of turning back the clock and finding that thinner human lurking inside, waiting to be released after years of overindulgence and underexertion. Perhaps this is the most tangible and noticeable effect. How could one deny that an improvement in mental attitude, energy level, mood, and sexual energy might follow the start of growth hormone therapy? However, before we stampede to our nearest anti-aging expert for a shot of growth hormone, let's look at the rest of the story.

Injecting GH can cause side effects in some patients such as edema, high blood pressure, arthralgia, and joint pains including carpal tunnel syndrome. Because of fluid retention, some patients may be at increased risk for congestive heart failure. In certain clinical situations, GH may worsen the effects of arthritis and diabetes. Typically, side effects can be reduced by lowering the dosage, but the optimum has not yet been established. Patients are usually started on an initial dose of 6 mcg/kg a day and may be gradually increased to 12.5 mcg/kg a day based on clinical response. If side effects do occur, the dosage should be halved. Initially, patients should be followed very closely, every one to two months, monitoring for fluid retention and glucose intolerance. Also, thyroid function must be checked since GH affects the metabolism of thyroid hormone. Over time, follow-up appointments can be reduced to three- or four-month intervals.

Another concern about rampant GH usage is the uncertainty about long-term effects. The National Institute of Aging in conjunction with the National Institutes of Health plans to release more comprehensive data on long-term GH usage, but not until the mid- to late 2000s. A 1998 study published in the *British Medical Journal* that followed close to 900 healthy men for 16 years found that those with the highest levels of GH also had the highest mortality rates. There is also speculation that GH may be a cofactor in the stimulation of tumor growth, so more research must be dedicated to this concern as well.

Last but not least, GH is not to be taken lightly, nor can it be taken cheaply. Prices vary upon the dosage, but a prescription of injectable GH can cost $12,000 to $15,000 per year. And that's not including preliminary blood work and monitoring, which can run to several thousands of dollars. Typically, these costs are not covered by insurance. But that doesn't stop thousands of entrepreneurs trying to promote growth hormone–like supplements or pills, which cost considerably less but have not been shown to be effective in the short or long term. In order to achieve the effects seen in the clinical studies with positive results, GH must be injected regularly. The molecules in the advertised oral supplements are typically broken down in the digestive tract and have no active ingredients that enter the bloodstream.

If you would like the effects of growth hormone, without the expense or potential risk, then exercise (see the discussion of the benefits of exercise earlier in this chapter). It has been proven that exercise itself is a growth hormone stimulant, helping your own body churn out bursts of this incredible natural anti-aging juice. Exercise mimics the benefits of growth hormone. Perhaps to some the only downfall is that we have to sweat to get results. On the other hand, if you are more inclined to sip from the potential fountain of youth, suffer from abdominal obesity, and hate to exercise, consult with an endocrinologist or certified anti-aging medical expert on the potential risks and benefits of GH therapy for your specific health and history. Short-term therapy may prove beneficial for a certain segment of the population.

DHEA

Dehydroepiandrosterone (DHEA) gained popularity in the mid 90s after a small clinical trial, published in the *Journal of Clinical Endocrinology and Metabolism,* found improvement in the physical and mental well-being of the middle-aged participants in the study. DHEA is an androgenic steroid, manufactured by the small adrenal glands that sit above our kidneys. Since it is an androgen, DHEA has more malelike hormone qualities. Despite the fact that the initial human study was characterized as "very preliminary, short term and without far-reaching conclusions," the results were touted by the lay press as a "miracle" and a new anti-aging wonder pill was born. Over time, even those who were swept away by the marvels of DHEA were finding some negative side effects, such as oily skin, hair loss, weight gain, acne, and irritability.

Even though DHEA is not found in food supplements, it is exempt from FDA regulation since it is categorized as a food supplement. But buyer beware. Because DHEA is a potent oral steroid that is not regulated, there are many who promote a multitude of presumed indications and benefits with varying strengths, potencies, and dosages. Women who were administered DHEA at a dose of 25 mg/day of oral micronized DHEA over a six-month study period were noted to have adverse lipid effects. Because of the possible effects of chronic administration of DHEA on subclinical prostate cancer or benign prostatic hyperplasia, men should be carefully monitored.

Potential Benefits of DHEA

There is no question that DHEA has been shown to extend the life-span of rats and mice and has even, at high doses, enhanced the immune system and prevented carcinogenesis in mice. But can this hormone actually extend the human life-span? Hopefully the answer will become available within this decade. The National Institutes of Health, the National Cancer Institute, and the National Institute on Aging are conducting research over a five-year period that will evaluate whether 50 mg a day of DHEA (when given to 100 men and 100 women in good health between the ages of 55 and 85) can actually reduce heart disease, cancer, diabetes, and improve weight loss in humans as effectively as it has in rodents. Early human studies have shown that 100 mg of oral DHEA given to elderly men and women can augment natural killer-cell toxicity and therefore enhance the aging immune system. Anything that can enhance the immune system also has the capacity to prolong life, for as the immune system deteriorates with age there is an increased incidence of atherosclerosis, autoimmune diseases, and cancer. Whether these preliminary findings result in actual clinical benefit remains to be answered, although these early studies are quite promising.

Many people take DHEA because of enhanced quality-of-life benefits. In the 1994 study by Dr. Samuel Yen and his researchers at the University of California, San Diego Department of Reproductive Medicine, published in the *Journal of Clinical Endocrinology and Metabolism,* the DHEA subjects reported better energy, better sleep, and better stress management than the placebo takers in the group. It has also been theorized that DHEA protects the body against the harmful effects of excess cortisol. When we are under stress our adrenal glands release large amounts of cortisol. Over time, chronic stress can result in high circulating levels of cortisol, which lead to age-related cellular damage. It has been theorized that DHEA can blunt excess levels of cortisol and protect the body from stress-induced damage. DHEA may also be cardioprotective in men. Preliminary studies by the Bowman Gray School of Medicine, published in the *Journal of the American Medical Association,* found that as DHEA levels went up, coronary artery disease in men went down.

DHEA can also protect the skeletal system. In a 12-month study using a topical form of DHEA (10 percent cream) in a population of postmenopausal women, significant increases were found in bone mineral density at the hip, while plasma bone alkaline phosphatase and urinary hydroxyproline, markers of bone breakdown, both decreased. Again, further studies are needed to support this preliminary but encouraging data.

If you are considering taking DHEA, be aware of what you are consuming. There are herbal products on the market claiming to contain DHEA. However, plants do not contain DHEA and plant substances marketed as the preliminary building blocks for DHEA do not have any measurable impact on circulating blood levels of DHEA. Commercial DHEA products are made from diosgenin, an extract of Mexican wild yam. Biochemists convert diosgenin to DHEA through chemical reactions, whereas the human body cannot convert diosgenin to DHEA. Products claiming to contain DHEA precursors or Mexican wild yam will not raise your DHEA levels. The published clinical research studies that showed DHEA's therapeutic effectiveness used real hormone, not yam extracts.

The best way to know if the product you are taking contains DHEA is to measure your own blood level before and after taking the supplement. Typically, if you are under age 35 or have normal DHEA levels, then DHEA supplements would not be recommended. In addition, men with prostate or testicular cancers and women with reproductive cancers (breast, ovarian, or uterine) should consult a physician before taking DHEA, which is a precursor to estrogen, progesterone, and testosterone.

Pregnenolone

Pregnenolone is a precursor to over 150 human steroid hormones, including DHEA, estrogen, progesterone, and testosterone. Steroid hormones are the fat-soluble hormones in the body. The adrenal glands manufacture pregnenolone from cholesterol. Cholesterol is the matriarch of our steroid hormone network. Following the production of pregnenolone, there is a rapid enzymatic conversion to progesterone, cortisol, corticosterone, aldosterone, DHEA, and smaller amounts of androstenedione, testosterone, and estradiol. Less clinically relevant scientific information is available about the precursor pregnenolene in comparison to its close cousin, DHEA; however, there are many believers in the miracles of this supplement as well as an abundance of anecdotal data.

Pregnenolone is considered a memory enhancer and is believed to help repair cells, especially in brain and nerve tissues. In rodents, the neurosteroid pregnenolone sulphate has been shown to have antidepressant effects. In humans, neurosteroids are steroids that arise de novo (anew) within the brain. Both pregnenolone and DHEA have been found in trace amounts in human brain cultures and are considered neurosteroids. The function of pregnenolone within the human brain is not fully understood, but it is believed by some to bring about a sense of well-being and protect cognitive functions.

Melatonin, Melancholy, and Mood

Melatonin is secreted by the pineal gland in the brain and is responsible for the regulation of our circadian rhythm. The release of melatonin is stimulated by darkness and suppressed by light. When our internal clock is disrupted by traveling across several time zones, it is not uncommon to experience insomnia, fatigue, irritability, and poor concentration, a condition more commonly known as jet lag. Melatonin has been found helpful in alleviating these symptoms. Similarly, when levels of melatonin diminish with age and sleep disturbances increase with age, it is thought that there is a connection between aging, diminishing melatonin secretion, poor sleep quality, and depressed mood. Elderly patients suffering from depression related to low melatonin levels (as in seasonal affective disorder) seem to benefit from melatonin supplements.

In very high pharmacological doses, melatonin works as an antioxidant. It has been speculated that the antioxidant effect can help prevent and treat some cancers by interfering with free radicals. However, it has been found that the antioxidant effect requires that melatonin levels over 100 times greater than the physiological melatonin secretion. Long-term side effects of such large dosing are unknown.

Living All the Days of Your Life

According to Ronald Klatz, D.O., president of the American Academy of Anti-Aging Medicine, patients who seek his care

> don't want to take aging lying down. They believe . . . and
> I agree . . . that they can avoid Alzheimer's disease, osteo-

arthritis, fatal heart attack and stroke. The technology is there to accomplish all of these things. Ultimately, anti-aging medicine seeks to create an ageless society where you can't distinguish with the naked eye between an average 65-year-old and a healthy and athletic 105-year-old, and we're seeing that right now.

Whether or not we can achieve an ageless society or a proactive health-oriented population remains to be determined. What we do know is that we can optimize our lives and our lifestyles by making adjustments in our diets, exercise routines, mental attitudes, and decisions in our personal life-enhancement strategies. We can speculate on the promise of new anti-aging miracles and scientific breakthroughs.

Anti-aging is the journey, living each day to the fullest is the ultimate destiny. However, by sharing our goals with our partner, we can make the quest for healthy longevity even more fulfilling and life enhancing. By achieving optimal living as a couple, each partner can become each other's coach and can harness the unique, irreplaceable elixir that love has to offer. Double menopause can then become exponentially better.

Bibliography

Angier, Natalie. 1999. *Woman: An Intimate Geography.* Boston: Houghton Mifflin.

Berman, Jennifer, M.D., and Laura Berman, Ph.D. 2001. *For Women Only: A Revolutionary Guide to Overcoming Sexual Dysfunction and Reclaiming Your Sex Life.* New York: Henry Holt.

Blaker, Karen, Ph.D. 1990. *Celebrating Fifty: Women Share Their Experiences, Challenges, and Insights on Becoming Fifty.* Chicago: Contemporary Books.

Bland, John H., M.D. 1997. *Live Long, Die Fast: Playing the Aging Game to Win.* Minneapolis: Fairview Press.

Block, Joel D., Ph.D., and Susan Crain Bakos. 1999. *Sex over 50.* Paramus, N.J.: Reward Books.

Blum, Deborah. 1997. *Sex on the Brain: The Biological Differences between Men + Women.* New York: Penguin.

Boteach, Shmuley. 1999. *Kosher Sex.* New York: Doubleday.

Brehony, Kathleen A. 1996. *Awakening at Midlife: Realizing Your Potential for Growth and Change.* New York: Riverhead Books.

Brody, Steve, Ph.D., and Kathy Brody, M.S. 1999. *Renew Your Mar-*

riage at Midlife: A Guide to Growing Together in Love. New York: G. P. Putnam's Sons.

Butler, Robert N., and Myrna I. Lewis. 1999. Sexuality and Aging. In *Principles of Geriatric Medicine and Gerontology,* ed. William R. Hazzard, M.D., John P. Blass, M.D., Ph.D., Walter H. Ettinger Jr., M.D. et al., 171–178. New York: McGraw-Hill.

Carter, Betty, M.S.W., and Joan K. Peters. 1996. *Love, Honor, and Negotiate: Building Partnerships That Last a Lifetime.* New York: Pocket Books.

Carter, Jean. 1995. *Stop Aging Now! The Ultimate Plan for Staying Young and Reversing the Aging Process.* New York: Harper-Collins.

Compton, Madonna Sophia, M.A. 1998. *Women at the Change: The Intelligent Woman's Guide to Menopause.* Saint Paul: Llewellyn Worldwide.

Crenshaw, Theresa L., M.D. 1996. *The Alchemy of Love and Lust.* New York: Putnam.

Cutter, Rebecca. 1994. *When Opposites Attract.* New York: Dutton Books.

Dabbs, James McBride, and Mary Godwin Dabbs. 2000. *Heroes, Rogues, and Lovers: Testosterone and Behavior.* New York: McGraw-Hill.

Daniluk, Judith C. 1998. *Women's Sexuality Across the Lifespan: Challenging Myths, Creating Meanings.* New York: Guilford Press.

DeFord, Deborah. 1997. *Are You Old Enough to Read This Book? Reflections on Mid-Life.* Pleasantville, N.Y.: Reader's Digest.

Diamond, Jed. 2000. *Surviving Male Menopause: A Guide for Women and Men.* Naperville, Ill.: Sourcebooks.

Durden-Smith, Jo, and Diane Desimone. 1983. *Sex and the Brain.* New York: Arbor House.

Dym, Barry, Ph.D., and Michael L. Glenn, M.D. 1993. *Couples: Exploring and Understanding the Cycles of Intimate Relationships.* New York: Harper Perennial.

Editors of Prevention Magazine Health Books. 1987. *Future Youth: How to Reverse the Aging Process.* Emmaus, Penn.: Rodale Press.

Friedan, Betty. 1993. *The Fountain of Age.* New York: Simon and Schuster.

Gerzon, Mark. 1996. *Listening to Midlife: Turning Your Crisis into a Quest.* Boston: Shambhala.

Godek, Gregory J. P. 1991. *1001 Ways to Be Romantic.* Boston: Casa Blanca Press.

Goldberg, Herb, Ph.D. 1987. *The Inner Male: Overcoming Roadblocks to Intimacy.* New York: New American Library.

Goldberg, Ken, M.D. 1999. *When the Man You Love Won't Take Care of His Health.* New York: Golden Books.

Goldstein, Irwin. 2000. Male Sexual Circuitry. *Scientific American* 8:70–75.

Goldstein, Steven R., and Laurie Ashner. 1998. *Could It Be Perimenopause?* Boston: Little, Brown.

Gottman, John, Ph.D. 1994. *Why Marriages Succeed or Fail . . . and How You Can Make Yours Last.* New York: Fireside Books.

Gottman, John M., Ph.D., and Nan Silver. 1999. *The Seven Principles for Making Marriage Work: A Practical Guide from the Country's Foremost Relationship Expert.* New York: Crown.

Handy, Bruce. 1994. The Viagra Praise. *Time,* May 4, 50–57.

Hayflick, Leonard, Ph.D. 1996. *How and Why We Age.* New York: Ballantine.

Helmstetter, Shad. 1990. *Finding the Fountain of Youth Inside Yourself.* New York: Pocket Books.

Hendricks, Gay. 1998. *Is the Ten-Second Miracle Creating Relationship Breakthroughs?* San Francisco: Harper Collins.

Holt, G. A., Ph.D., R.Ph., M. McCrory, Ed.D., G. Norris, M.D., and J. Sandler, Ph.D. 1997. *Extend Your Lifespan: How You Can Live a Long and Healthy Life.* Tampa: Mancorp.

Huston, James E., M.D. 1998. *Menopause: A Guide to Health and Happiness.* New York: Facts on File.

Jung, C. G. 1989. *Aspects of the Masculine.* Trans. R. F. C. Hull. Princeton, N.J. Princeton University Press.

Keough, Carol, ed., and Editors of Prevention Magazine Health Books. 1987. *Future Youth: How to Reverse the Aging Process.* Emmaus, Penn.: Rodale Press.

Klatz, Ronald, and Robert Goldman. 1996. *Stopping the Clock.* New Canaan, Conn.: Keats Publishing.

Lacayo, Richard. 2000. Are You Man Enough? *Time,* April 24, 58–64.

Landau, Carol, Ph.D., Michele G. Cyr, M.D., and Anne W. Moulton, M.D. 1994. *The Complete Book of Menopause.* New York: Perigee Books.

Leiblum, Sandra R., Ph.D., and Raymond C. Rosen, Ph.D., eds. 2000. *Principles and Practice of Sex Therapy.* 3rd ed. New York: Guilford Press.

Lenz, Elinor. 1993. *Rights of Passage: How Women Can Find a New Freedom in Their Mid Years.* Los Angeles: Lowell House.

Levinson, Daniel J. 1978. *The Seasons of a Man's Life.* New York: Ballantine Books.

———. 1996. *The Seasons of a Woman's Life.* New York: Ballantine Books.

Lobo, Rogerio A. 1999. *Treatment of the Post-Menopausal Woman: Basic and Clinical Aspects.* Philadelphia: Lippincott, Williams, and Wilkins.

Mahoney, David, and Richard Restak, M.D. 1998. *Longevity Strategy.* New York: John Wiley and Sons.

Mandell, Judy. 1998. *What to Expect in Your Fifties: A Woman's Guide to Health, Vitality, and Longevity.* New York: Dell.

Marshel, Judy E., M.B.A., R.D., and Linda Konner. 1998. *Trouble-Free Menopause: Manage Your Symptoms and Your Weight.* New York: Avon Books.

Maslin, Bonnie, Ph.D. 1994. *The Angry Marriage: Overcoming the Rage, Reclaiming the Love.* New York: Hyperion Books.

Medina, John J. 1996. *The Clock of Ages: Why We Age, How We Age, and Winding Back the Clock.* Cambridge, England: Cambridge University Press.

Meilahn, Elaine, Dr.Ph., and Ian H. Thorneycroft, M.D., Ph.D. 2001. Prevention of Heart Disease in Women: Is Postmenopausal Estrogen Therapy Warranted? *Menopause Management* 10(4): 16–28.

Moir, Anne, Ph.D., and David Jessel. 1991. *Blame Sex: The Real Difference Between Men and Women.* New York: Delta Books.

Moore, Thomas. 1994. *Soul Mates: Honoring the Mysteries of Love and Relationship.* New York: Harper Perennial.

———. 1998. *The Soul of Sex: Cultivating Life as an Act of Love.* New York: HarperCollins.

Muir, Charles, and Carolyn Muir. 1989. *Tantra: The Art of Conscious Loving.* San Francisco: Mercury House.

Nichols, Michael P., Ph.D. 1995. *The Lost Art of Listening: How Learning to Listen Can Improve Relationships.* New York: Guilford Press.

Olshansky, S. Jay, and Bruce A. Carnes. 2001. *The Quest for Immortality: Science at the Frontiers of Aging.* New York: W. W. Norton.

Osing, Richard A. 1998. *Love at Midlife: Building and Rebuilding Relationships at Midlife.* San Francisco: Rudi.

Pogrebin, Letty Cottin. 1996. *Getting Over Getting Older: An Intimate Journey.* New York: Berkley Books.

Polston, Betty L., Ph.D., and Susan K. Golant, M.A. 1999. *Loving Midlife Marriage: A Guide to Keeping Romance Alive from the Empty-Nest through Retirement.* New York: John Wiley and Sons.

Reichman, Judith. M.D. 1998. *I'm Not in the Mood: What Every Woman Should Know about Improving Her Libido.* New York: William Morrow.

Roth, Dick. 1999. *"No, It's Not Hot in Here": A Husband's Guide to Understanding Menopause.* East Sandwich, Mass.: North Star Publications.

Sachs, Judith. 1994. *The Healing Power of Sex.* Englewood Cliffs, N.J.: Prentice Hall.

Schnarch, David, Ph.D. 1997. *Passionate Marriage: Keeping Love and Intimacy Alive in Committed Relationships.* New York: Henry Holt.

Sheehy, Gail. 1995. *New Passages: Mapping Your Life Across Time.* New York: Random House.

————. 1998. *Understanding Men's Passages: Discovering the New Map of Men's Lives.* New York: Random House.

Shoenberg, Fred. 1987. *Middle Age Rage . . . and Other Male Indignities.* New York: Simon and Schuster.

Singer, June. 1994. *Boundaries of the Soul: The Practice of Jung's Psychology.* New York: Anchor Books.

Tenover, Lisa J., M.D., Ph.D. 1998. Male Hormone Replacement Therapy Including "Andropause." *Endocrinology and Metabolism Clinics of North America* 27(4):969–987.

————. 1999. Testosterone Replacement Therapy in Older Adult Men. *International Journal of Andrology* 22:300–306.

————. 1999. Trophic Factors and Male Hormone Replacement. In *Principles of Geriatric Medicine and Gerontology,* ed. William R. Hazzard, M.D., John P. Blass, M.D., Ph.D., Walter H. Ettinger Jr., M.D., et al., 1029–1040. New York: McGraw-Hill.

Thoele, Susan Patton. 1998. *Freedoms after Fifty.* Berkeley, Calif.: Conarie Press.

Utian, Wulf H., M.D., Ph.D., and Ruth S. Jacobowitz. 1990. *Managing Your Menopause.* New York: Fireside Books.

Walford, Roy L., and Lisa Walford. 1994. *The Anti-Aging Plan: Strategies and Recipes for Extending Your Healthy Years.* New York: Four Walls Eight Windows.

Warga, Claire, Ph.D. 1999. *Menopause and the Mind.* New York: Free Press.

Zilbergeld, Bernie, Ph.D. 1999. *The New Male Sexuality: The Truth about Men, Sex, and Pleasure.* New York: Bantam.

References

AARP/*Modern Maturity.* 1999. *Sexuality Study.*

Arlt, W., J. Haas, F. Calies, et al. 1999. Biotransformation of Oral Dehydroepiandrosterone in Elderly Men: Significant Increase in Circulating Estrogens. *Journal of Endocrinology and Metabolism* 84(6):2170–2176.

Bachmann, M.D., Gloria A., ed. 1999. Role of Androgens in the Menopause. *American Journal of Obstetrics and Gynecology* 180(Supplement):S308–S340.

Barnhart, K. T., E. Freeman, J. A. Grisso, D. J. Rader, et al. 1999. The Effect of Dehydroepiandrosterone Supplementation to Symptomatic Perimenopausal Women on Serum Endocrine Profiles, Lipid Parameters, and Health Related Quality of Life. *Journal of Clinical Endocrinology and Metabolism* 84(11): 3896–3902.

Basson, R., J. Berman, A. Burnett, et al. 2000. Report of the International Consensus Development Conference on Female Sexual Dysfunction: Definitions and Classifications. *Journal of Urology* 163:888–893.

Bhasin, Shalender. 2000. The Dose Dependent Effects of Testosterone on Sexual Function and on Muscle Mass and Function. *Mayo Clinic Proceedings* 75(supplement):S70–S76.

Blakely, J. A. 2000. The Heart and Estrogen/Progestin Replacement Study Revisited *Archives of Internal Medicine* 160:2897–2900.

Burr, M. L., A. M. Fehily, J. F. Gilbert et al. 1989. Effects of Changes in Fat, Fish and Fibre Intakes on Death and Myocardial Reinfarction. *Lancet* 2:757–761.

Butcher, Josi. 1999. Female Sexual Problems: Loss of Desire. *British Medical Journal* 318:41–43.

Callies, F. 2000. Influence of Oral Dehydroepiandrosterone (DHEA) on Urinary Steroid Metabolized in Males and Females. *Steroids* 65(2):98–102.

Cutler, Winnifred E., Ph.D., and Elizabeth Genovese-Stone, M.D. 1998. Wellness in Women After Forty Years of Age: The Role of Sex Hormones and Pheromones. *Diseases a Month* 44(9):423–546.

Evan-Simpson, Rurn, Gary Rubin, and Colin Clyne, et al. 2000. The Role of Global Estrogen Biosynthesis in Males and Females. *Trends in Endocrinology and Metabolism* 11(5):184–188.

Faustini-Fustini, Marco, Vincenzo Rochira, and Cesare Carani. 1999. Oestrogen Deficiency in Men: Where Are We Today? *European Journal of Endocrinology* 140:111–129.

Feldman, H. A., I. Goldstein, D. G. Hatzichristou, et al. 1994. Impotence and Its Medical and Psychological Correlates: Results of the Massachusetts Male Aging Study. *Journal of Urology* 151(1):54–61.

Flynn, D. Weaver-Osterholtz, M. A., K. L. Sharpe-Timms, et al. 1999. Dehydroepiandrosterone Replacement in Aging Humans. *Journal of Endocrinology and Metabolism* 84(5):1527–1533.

Ford, D. E., L. A. Mead, P. P. Chang, et al. 1998. Depression Is a Risk Factor for Coronary Artery Disease in Men. *Archives of Internal Medicine* 158:1422–1426.

Francis, R. M. 1999. The Effects of Testosterone on Osteoporosis in Men. *Clinical Endocrinology* 50:411–414.

Gambacciani, Marco, and Massimo Ciaponi. 2000. Postmenopausal Osteoporosis Risk Management. *Current Opinions in Obstetrics and Gynecology* 12:189–197.

Gonzalez-Bono, E., A. Salvador, M. A. Serrano, and J. Ricarte, 1999. Testosterone, Cortisol, and Mood in a Sports Team Competition. *Hormones and Behavior* 35:55–62.

Hofbauer, Lorenz C., and Sundeep Khosla. 1999. Androgen Effects on Metabolism: Recent Progress and Controversies. *European Journal of Endocrinology* 140:271–286.

Hoffman, Ronald, 1996. *Advances in Anti-Aging Medicines.* Vol. 1 of *Endocrine Aspects of Aging,* 43–51. New York: Mary Ann Liebert.

Hollosy, John O., M.D. 2000. The Biology of Aging. *Mayo Clinic Proceedings* 75(Supplement):S3–S9.

Hu, F. B., M. J. Stampfer, J. E. Manson, et al. 1998. Frequent Nut Consumption and Risk of Coronary Heart Disease in Women: Prospective Cohort Study. *British Medical Journal* 317:1341–1345.

Inzucchi, Silvio F. 1997. Growth Hormone in Adults: Indications and Implications. *Hospital Practice* (January 15):79–96.

Iqbal, Mohammad Masud, M.D., M.Ph., M.S.Ph. 2000. Osteoporosis: Epidemiology, Diagnosis, and Treatment. *Southern Medical Journal* 93:2–18.

Jancin, Bruce. 2001. Progestins Plus Estrogen Add to Breast Cancer Risk. *Internal Medicine News* (March 1):16.

———. 2001. Soy Strikes Out for the Treatment of Hot Flashes and Breast Cancer. *Internal Medicine News* (March 1):18.

Jannini, E. A., E. Screponi, E. Carosa, et al. 1999. Lack of Sexual Activity from Erectile Dysfunction Is Associated with a Reversible Reduction in Serum Testosterone. *International Journal of Andrology* 22:385–392.

Jensen, Michael D. 2000. Androgen Effects on Body Composition and Fat Metabolism. *Mayo Clinic Proceedings* 75(Supplement): S65–S70.

Kohn, Ira, M.D., and Steven Kaplan, M.D. 2000. Female Sexual Dysfunction: What Is Known? *Contemporary Obstetrics and Gynecology* 2:25–46.

Krystal, Andrew D., M.D., M.S. 2001. Insomnia in Peri-Menopausal and Post-Menopausal Women. *Geriatric Times* (May–June): 21–23.

Lambing, Sheryl L. 2000. Osteoporosis Prevention, Detection, and Treatment: A Mandate for Primary Care Physicians. *Postgraduate Medicine* 107(7):37–56.

Lanier, William, M.D., ed. 2000. Symposium on Testosterone Replacement in Elderly Men. *Mayo Clinic Proceedings* 75(Supplement):S1–S91.

LeBlanc, E. S., M.D., M.Ph., J. Janowsky, Ph.D., B. K. S. Chan, M. S., and H. D. Nelson, M.D., M.Ph. 2001. Hormone Replacement Therapy and Cognition: Systematic Review and Meta-Analysis. *Journal of the American Medical Association* 285(11):1489–1499.

Lee, Robert, and Marjorie Casebier. 1971. *The Spouse Gap: Weathering the Marriage Crisis During Middlescence.* Nashville, Tenn. Abingdon Press.

Lotufo, Paulo A., M.D., Dr.P.H. Claudia U. Chae, M.D., Umed A. Ajani, M.B.P.S., M.P.H., et al. 2000. Male Pattern Baldness and Coronary Heart Disease: Physicians Health Study. *Archives of Internal* Medicine 160(2):165–171.

Lundberg, Gary, and Joy Lundberg, 2001. *Married for Better. Not Worse: The Fourteen Secrets to a Happy Marriage.* New York: Viking Press.

Mair, K. Sreekumaran, M.D., Shalender Bhasin, M.D., John E. Morley, M.D., et al., eds. 2000. The Pros and Cons of Testosterone Replacement in Elderly Men: A Panel Discussion. *Mayo Clinic Proceedings* 75(Supplement):S88–S91.

Maison P., B. Balkau, D. Simon, et al. 1998. Growth Hormone as a Risk for Premature Mortality in Healthy Subjects: Data from the Paris Prospective Study. *British Medical Journal* 316:1132–1133.

Manson, JoAnn E., M.D., Dr.P.H., and Kathryn A. Martin. 2001. Postmenopausal Hormone Replacement Therapy. *New England Journal of Medicine* 345:34–40.

Matthews, Karen A., and Jane Cauley. 1999. Menopause and Midlife Health Changes. In *Principles of Geriatric Medicine and Gerontology*, ed. William R. Hazzard, M.D., John P. Blass, M.D., Ph.D., Walter H. Ettinger Jr., M.D., et al. New York: McGraw-Hill.

Mazza, E., M. Maccario, J. Ramunni, et al. 1999. Dehydroepiandrosterone Sulfate Levels in Women: Relationships with Age, Body Mass Index, and Insulin Levels. *Journal of Endocrinological Investigations* 22(9):681–687.

Morales, A. J., R. H. Haubrich, J. Y. Hwang, H. Asakura, and S. S. Yen. 1998. The Effect of Six Months Treatment with a 100-Milligram Daily Dose of Dehydroepiandrosterone (DHEA) on Circulating Sex Steroids, Body Composition, and Muscle Strength in Age-Advanced Men and Women. *Clinical Endocrinology (Oxford)* 49(4):421–432.

Morales, Albaro, Jeremy P. W. Heaton, and Coloey C. Carson III. 2000. Andropause: A Misnomer for a True Clinical Entity. *Journal of Urology* 163:705–712.

Morley, J. E., M.B., B.C.H., 2000. Testosterone Replacement and the Physiologic Aspects of Aging in Men. *Mayo Clinic Proceedings* 75(Supplement):S83–S87.

Morley, J. E., E. Charlton, P. Patrick, et al. 2000. Validation of a Screening Questionnaire for Androgen Deficiency in Aging Males. *Metabolism* 49:1239–1242.

Mosca, Lori, M.D., Ph.D., Scott M. Grundy, M.D., Ph.D., and Debra Judelson, M.D., et al. 1999. Guide to Preventive Cardiology for Women. *Circulation* 99:2480–2484.

Nehra, Ajay, M.D. 2000. Treatment of Endocrinologic Male Sexual Dysfunction. *Mayo Clinic Proceedings* 75(Supplement):S40–S45.

Nieschlag, E., and H. M. Behre, eds. 1997. *Andrology: Male Reproductive Health and Dysfunction.* Berlin: Springer.

Oudshoorn, N. E. J. 1997. Menopause, Only for Women? The Social Construction of Menopause as an Exclusively Female Condition. *Journal of Psychosomatic Obstetrics and Gynecology* 18:137–144.

Phillips, Nancy A., M.D. 2000. Female Sexual Dysfunction: Evaluation and Treatment. *American Family Physician* 62(1):127–136.

Robertson, R. M. 2001. Women and Cardiovascular Disease: The Risks of Misperception and the Need for Action. *Circulation* 103:2318.

Rudman, D., A. Feller, H. Nagra, et al. 1990. Effects of Human Growth Hormone in Men Over 60 Years Old. *New England Journal of Medicine* 323:1–6.

Sarrel, P. M., and M. I. Whitehead. 1985. Sex and Menopause: Defining the Issues. *Maturitas* 7:217–224.

Seifer, David B., M.D., and Elizabeth A. Kennard. 1999. *Menopause: Endocrinology and Management.* Totowa, N.J.: Humana Press.

Sherwin, B. B. 1988. Estrogen and/or Androgen Replacement Therapy and Cognitive Functioning in Surgically Menopausal Women. *Psychoneuroendocrinology* 10:325–335.

Skolnick, A. A. 1996. Medical News and Perspectives: Scientific Verdict Still Out on DHEA. *Journal of the American Medical Association* 276:1365–1367.

Smith, D. S. Frankel, J. Yarnell. 1997. Sex and Death: Are They Still Related? Findings from the Caerphilly Cohort Study. *British Medical Journal* 315(7123):1641–1644.

Tenover, Lisa J., M.D. 2000. Experience With Testosterone Replacement in the Elderly. *Mayo Clinic Proceedings* 75(Supplement):S77–S82.

Tilbis, R. S., M. Kahonen, and M. Harkonen. 1999. Dehydroepi-androsterone Sulfate, Diseases and Mortality in a General Aged Population. *Aging (Milano)* 11(1):30–34.

Vermeulen, A. 2001. Androgen Replacement Therapy in the Aging Male: A Critical Evaluation. *Journal of Clinical Endocrinology and Metabolism* 86(6):2380–2390.

Voelkel, Rebecca. 2000. Hormonal Confusion Creates "Credibility Gap." *Journal of the American Medical Association* 284(4):424–428.

Wang, C., G. Alexander, N. Berman, et al. 1996. Testosterone Replacement Therapy Improves Mood in Hypogonadal Men: A Clinical Research Center Study. *Journal of Clinical Endocrinology and Metabolism* 81(10):3578–3583.

Woodhouse, L. J., S. L. Asa, S. G. Thomas, and S. Ezzat. 2001. Growth Hormone Deficiency and Physical Function. *Journal of Clinical Endocrinology and Metabolism* 86(4):1839–1840.

Index

AARP, 68–69
abdominal girth, increased, 107,
    201–202, 210
abortions, 77, 147
acknowledging midlife hormonal
    changes, 51, 61
    of spouse, 14, 181–82
ADAM (androgen decline in the aging
    male), *see* male menopause
aerobic exercise, *see* exercise
affairs, 12, 48, 50, 68, 110, 121, 133,
    135, 156–57, 168
    cyberaffair, 182–84
    surviving your husband's midlife,
        136–37
    suspicion of, 87, 112
affection, practicing random acts of,
    125–26
aging, 194
    attitudes and fears about, 112–14
    erections and, 87, 90
    the truth about anti-aging, *see* anti-
        aging

alcohol, 33, 54, 62, 88, 139
Allen, Woody, 58
All in the Family, 22–23
Alzheimer's disease, 32
American Academy of Anti-Aging
    Medicine, 216
American College of Nutrition, 201
American Heart Association, 35, 37
Anafranil, 78
andropause, *see* male menopause
anger, 53, 54, 140–41, 178
    getting rid of, 123–24
angina, 202
angiography, 36
angioplasty, 86
anima and animus, 102–104
anti-aging, 193–217
    abdominal girth, losing, 201–202
    avoiding boredom and negativity,
        207
    creativity, 205–206
    diet and, 197–201
    examples of strategies for, 195

anti-aging *(continued)*
  exercise and, 201, 202–205
  humor and laughter and, 206–207
  longevity quotient (LQ)
    questionnaire, 195–96
  maximizing your personal longevity
    quotient (LQ), 197–208
  meditation and, 208
  mental exercise, 205
  reducing stress, 207–208
  sex and, 205
  staying connected, 207
  superhormones, 208–16
antidepressants, 77, 79, 89, 95, 215
antioxidants, 152, 167, 200, 216
anxiety, 89, 152, 202
  female menopause and, 32, 155
  male menopause and, 48, 107
appreciating your partner, 120–21,
    151–52, 158, 172–73
arthritis, 199, 211
"Art of Conscious Loving, The," 189
Astroglide, 75, 150
atherosclerosis, 86, 88, 214
Ativan, 78
atorvastatin, 38
attractiveness, *see* body image
autoimmune diseases, 214

back pain, 204
balance, building, 34–35, 204–205
barrier methods of contraception, 151
Beatty, Warren, 58
bedtime, synchronizing, 114–17
bedtime stories, sharing, 172
Bellow, Saul, 16, 58
benign prostatic hyperplasia (BPH), 96
beta-blocking drugs, 36
beta-endorphins, 89
birth control pills, low-dose, 77, 147,
    151
bisphosphonates, 34

blame, avoiding, 185
blood clots, 199
blood pressure, 39, 42, 98
  hypertension, 88, 202, 208, 211
  optimal, 38
blood sugar, 198
body image, 69, 78, 108, 133, 151–52,
    156, 158
body mass, loss of lean, 94, 210
  female menopause and, 16
  male menopause and, 16, 52
body mass index (BMI), 39
body weight, 39, 90, 178, 203
  ideal, 198
bone density, 76, 94, 95, 214
  female menopause, 33–35
  male menopause and, 16, 52
  osteoporosis, *see* osteoporosis
  testing, 33–34
boredom, 207
*Boundaries of the Soul: The Practice
    of Jung's Psychology* (Jung), 103
Bowman Gray School of Medicine,
    214
brain:
  keeping mentally active, 205
  pregnenolone and, 215–16
breast cancer, 35, 95, 200, 215
Bridges of Madison County, The
    (Waller), 170
Brigham and Women's Hospital, 39
British Medical Journal, 211
Burr, Dr. M. L., 199–200

calcitonin, 34
calcium, 33, 34, 152
caloric restriction, 197–99
cancer, 42, 58, 198, 199, 200, 214, 216
  in females, 35, 36
  see also specific types of cancer
carbohydrates, processed, 197
carbonated beverages, 33

cardiovascular disease, 41, 167, 198, 199, 214
 abdominal girth and, 201–202
 erectile dysfunction (ED) and, 86, 88, 89
 female, 21, 35–40
 male, 52
 prevention of, 36–40
 sexuality and, 78, 80
 testosterone supplementation and, 94–95
carpal tunnel syndrome, 211
celebrations, impromptu, 171
celebrities:
 becoming fathers after 50, 16, 58
 female menopause and, 22, 157
Census Bureau, 51
challenges and changes, handling, 175–92
 accepting, 184
 communication for, 175–77, 184, 185, 191
 four ways to wreck a long-term relationship, 177–84
 second honeymoon, 187–89
 taking stock of your relationship, 186–87
 Tantra, 189–90
 tips for building a healthy midlife relationship, 184–86
chi gung, 204
children leaving home, 120, 132–35, 133–34, 163, 173
 male menopause and, 56–57
chocolate, 167
cholesterol, dietary, 215
cholesterol levels, serum, 39, 42, 95
 cardiovascular disease and, 36
 HDL, 37, 38, 95, 97, 167, 199, 202
 LDL, 37, 38, 95, 97, 202
 medications to lower, 36
 testing, 90

circadian rhythm, 216
Circulation, 35
circulatory system, 202, 203
Clinton, Bill, 50, 183
Clinton, Hillary Rodham, 50
coffee, 33
cognitive function, 32
colon cancer, 52
commitment, 186
Commonwealth Fund, 51
communication, 62–63, 112, 158, 175–77, 184, 185, 191
 couple office visits and, 17, 111
 intimacy and, 114
 lack of, 12, 13
 with physicians, 43
 about sex, 68, 73, 82–83, 110–11, 140, 150–51
compassion, 184, 185
concentration:
 female menopause and, 145, 146, 181
 male menopause and, 2
constipation, 197
contraception, 151
cortisol, 214, 215
counseling, 141, 179
creativity, 205–206
critical, being, 177–79
cultural differences in menopause experience, 31

danger zones, questionnaire for identifying, 9–11
dates, pretend, 171–72
death or illness of a peer, 54–55, 59, 134, 163
denial:
 of erectile dysfunction (ED), 85–86, 87, 110
 of male menopause, 59–60, 86, 107

depression, 54, 170
  antidepressants, 77, 79, 89, 95, 216
  erectile dysfunction and, 89
  female menopause and, 32, 79
  female sexuality and, 78
  male menopause and, 16, 47, 48, 53,
    55, 107, 137–39, 140, 179
  melatonin supplements for, 216
  testosterone supplementation and,
    76
DHEA (dehydroepiandrosterone),
  212–16
diabetes, 52, 88, 199, 202, 211
  type 2, 201, 202
diet, 48, 53, 111, 112, 152
  caloric restriction, 197–99
  cardiovascular disease and, 38–40
  longevity and, 197–99
  mini-meal approach, 39–40, 152
  osteoporosis and, 33
diosgenin, 214–15
disdain, 179–80
divorce, 1, 12, 18, 56, 163, 166, 170,
  187
drug abuse, 88, 139
drug interactions, 42
dual-energy x-ray absorptiometry
  (DEXA), 34
dyspareunia, 81, 155

educating yourself about midlife
  hormonal changes, 14
Effexor, 89
ejaculation, 87, 90, 140
Elavil, 78
emotional intimacy, *see* intimacy
emotions, controlling, 46–48, 138, 141
empowerment, 157
empty-nest syndrome, *see* children
  leaving home
endometriosis, 24
endorphins, 165, 168

energy levels, 40, 54, 77, 79, 111, 152,
  203
  see also fatigue
erectile dysfunction (ED), 48, 52, 107,
  110, 135, 140
  physical causes of, 86–88
  psychological causes of, 88–89
  self-doubt and denial of, 85–86, 87,
    110
  statistics, 87
  testosterone supplementation and,
    54
  as trigger of male menopause, 56–57
  Viagra and, 4, 90
erection:
  aging and, 87, 90
  erectile dysfunction, *see* erectile
    dysfunction (ED)
  visual stimulation and, 69
essential fatty acids, 197, 199
estradiol, 21, 28
Estring, 155
estrogen, 167, 215
  female menopause and, 16, 27
  HRT, *see* hormone replacement
    therapy (HRT)
  in perimenopause, 146
  protective functions of, 32–33
  roles of, 153
exercise, 48, 79, 89, 111, 112, 113–14,
  141, 146, 147, 152, 178, 201–205,
  209, 212
  bone density and, 33, 202
  to build balance, 34–35, 204–205
  cardiovascular disease and, 36,
    37–38, 202
  depression and, 139, 202
  for flexibility, 152, 204
  strength training, 33, 113, 202–203

falling in love, 164–65
falls in the elderly, 34–35, 204

family medical history, 41–42
fathers, midlife, 16, 58
fatigue, 16, 48, 107
fats, dietary, 39, 53, 197, 198, 199, 200
  low-fat cooking methods, 199
faultfinding, 177–79
female menopause, 21–43
  average age of, 108, 153
  celebrities and, 22, 157
  definition of, 153
  hormonal changes, *see* estrogen, female menopause and; testosterone, female menopause and
  hormone replacement therapy, *see* hormone replacement therapy (HRT)
  life expectancy and, 21
  man's guide to surviving his woman's, *see* man's guide to surviving his woman's midlife change
  in 1900s, 21
  in 1950s, 22, 40
  openness about, 21–22
  perimenopause, *see* perimenopause
  seven essential facts about, 108–109
  symptoms of, *see specific symptoms*
fertility, 16, 153
fiber, 39, 199
fifty, turning, 153
fish and fish oils, 197, 199–200
flexibility, 185
  physical, 152, 204
fluoxymesterone, 96
fMRI (functional magnetic resonance imaging), 30
folic acid, 38
Fonda, Jane, 157
Food and Drug Administration, 97, 209, 213

foot massage, 172
Ford, Dr. Daniel, 89
Fosamax, 34
free radicals, 197–98, 216
friendship(s), 207
  after retirement, 63
  intimacy and, 114, 121–22
  renewing your, 141–42
fruits, 39, 197, 199
FSH (follicle-stimulating hormone), 28, 29, 92, 93
fuzzy-headedness, 145, 155, 181

Gabor, Eva, 34
genisten, 200
Gerontology Research Laboratory, UCLA School of Medicine, 197
GH (growth hormone), 208–12
Giuliani, Rudolph, 58
glucocorticoid steroids, 209
Graham, Katharine, 34–35, 204
Grandma Moses, 205–206
grandparent, becoming a, 57–58
growth hormone (GH), 208–12
growth hormone-releasing hormone (GHRH), 209
gynecomastia, 96

happiness factor, 53
Harris and Associates, Louis, 51
Harvard Medical School, 39
Hawn, Goldie, 22, 157
headaches, 145, 146, 147, 208
head trauma, 34, 204
health crisis, male menopause precipitated by, 58–59
Heart and Estrogen/Progestin Replacement Study (HERS), 37
heart attack, 35, 36, 37, 38, 42, 97, 200, 202, 208

heart disease, *see* cardiovascular disease
herbal remedies, 42, 152, 214
hip fractures, 34, 95, 202, 204
hippocampus, 32, 33
Hippocrates, 203
hobbies, 62, 63, 106, 136
Holmes, John Andrew, 119
Holmes, Oliver Wendell, Sr., 113
homocysteine, 38
honeymoon:
  nostalgia, reviving, 169
  second, 173, 187–89
hormone replacement therapy (HRT), 11–12, 26, 152
  Alzheimer's disease and, 32
  cardiovascular disease and, 36–37
  celebrity proponents of, 22
  deciding on, 41–43
  media coverage of, 30
  osteoporosis and, 34
hot flashes:
  chills after, 26
  cultural differences, 31
  female menopause and, 16, 17, 21, 22, 23, 24–29, 31, 108, 145, 146, 147, 149, 152, 153–54
  male menopause and, 2, 107
  as neuroendocrine event, 28
  research on, 24–29
  surgical menopause and, 27–28
  triggers of, 149, 154
  variation of experience of, 28–29, 53–54
  as vasomotor event, 29
humor, 38, 206–207
Hutton, Lauren, 22, 157
hypertension, 88, 202, 208, 211
hyperthyroidism medications, 33
hypoestrogenization, 81
hypothalamus, 28, 92
hysterectomy, 27–28, 75, 77, 147

identifying double-menopause danger zones, questionnaire for, 9–11
immune system, 198, 202, 208
  DHEA and, 213–14
incontinence, 78
indecisiveness, 107
independence, 136
informed consent, 24–25
insulin, 198
intimacy, 185
  balancing togetherness and space, 124–25
  friendship and, 114, 121–22
  getting rid of anger and resentment, 123–24
  making a conscious decision to reconnect, 119–20
  practicing random acts of affection, 125–26
  questionnaire, 117–19
  sensitivity to each other's needs and, 122–23
  synchronizing bedtime, 114–17
in vitro fertilization (IVF), 24
irritability, 54, 78, 170
  female menopause and, 32, 154, 155
  male menopause and, 48, 53, 107, 138, 140, 141
irritable bowel syndrome, 208
isoflavones, 31

Japanese, the, 31, 199, 200, 201
job loss, 54–55
Johns Hopkins University, 89
Journal of Clinical Endocrinology and Metabolism, 200–201, 212, 214
Journal of the American Medical Association, 214
Journal of Urology, 87
Jungian psychology, 103

King, Larry, 16, 58
Klatz, Ronald, 216–17
K-Y jelly, 75

Lancet, 199–200
Lander, Dr. Nedra, 51–52
laughter, 38, 206–207
"Lawyers on Love," 166
Lewinsky, Monica, 50, 183
Leydig cells, 92
LH (luteinizing hormone), 28, 29, 92, 93
libido, loss of, 77–78
  antidepressants and, 77–78, 89
  erectile dysfunction and, 90
  female menopause and, 17, 67, 68, 74–82, 108, 111, 145, 146, 156, 181
  male menopause and, 16, 48, 91–92, 111, 140
  testosterone supplementation and, 54, 75–76, 94, 95
Librium, 22, 40
life expectancy, 21, 193–94
listening, 157–58, 185
Lobo, Dr. Rogerio, 144
longevity quotient (LQ):
  maximizing your, 197–208
  questionnaire, 195–96
love, 186
love notes, 172

MacArthur, General Douglas, 113, 193
male climactgeric, *see* male menopause
male menopause:
  action steps for men, 51–54
  age range for experiencing, 4, 46
  andropause, referred to as, 2, 3, 15
  denial and, 59–60, 86, 107
  factors that may precipitate, 54–59, 132–34

fertility and, 16
information available about, vii, 1
lack of awareness about, 2–3, 12–13, 45, 107, 181
male physicians and, 3, 45, 60, 107
questionnaire, 49–50
seven essential facts about, 107–108
spouse's role and, 60–63
suffering in silence, 46–48
support groups, 3
symptoms of, *see specific symptoms*
testosterone levels and, *see* testosterone, male menopause and
woman's guide to surviving her man's, *see* woman's guide to surviving her man's midlife change
male pattern baldness, 52
man's guide to surviving his woman's midlife change, 143–59
  dealing with perimenopause, 143–47
  determining if your partner is entering perimenopause, 147–49
  helping your partner get through perimenopause, 148–53
  what every man should know, 153–57
  what every woman wishes her man knew, 157–59
Massachusetts Male Aging Study, 87
massage, 170, 172
Masters, Dr. William, 111
Maxilube, 75
media coverage of menopause, 30
meditation, 38, 208
melatonin, 216
memories, reviving romantic, 169
memory, 30, 215
  estrogen and, 32
  female menopause and, 32, 155
Men's Health, 166

menstruation:
  changes in, 16, 108, 143, 146, 147,
    149
  emotional effects on, 14–15
mental exercise, 205
mentoring, 63
metabolism, 202–203
methyltestosterone, 75–76, 96–97
Mexican wild yam, 215
midlife couples:
  danger zones, questionnaire for
    identifying, 9–11
  divorce among, *see* divorce
  handling challenges and changes,
    see challenges and changes,
    handling
  intimacy, moving toward greater,
    114–26
  medical consultations, going
    together for, 2, 16–17, 107–108,
    111, 150
  mission statement for, 104–107
  perceptions about changes in each
    other, 13
  private fears of, 110–14
  romance, *see* romance, midlife
  sexuality of, *see* sexuality, midlife
  strengthening their relationship, 19
  time apart and time together,
    balancing, 106, 124–25, 159, 174
  see also midlife crisis
midlife crisis:
  new perspective on, 100
  as opportunity or dilemma, 100–102
  as a turning point, 99–100, 104
midlife sexuality, female perspective
    of, 67–83, 108, 145, 155–56,
    158
  common changes, 67
  cultural messages about, 80–81
  physicians and, 67, 68, 82–83
  quiz, 70–73

  sex as undesirable, 80–82
  Viagra and, 90–91
midlife sexuality, male perspective of,
    68–69, 85–98
  erectile dysfunction, *see* erectile
    dysfunction (ED)
  feelings and, 98
  sexual desire versus sexual function,
    91–92
  testosterone and, *see* testosterone
mission statement, midlife, 104–107
Modern Maturity, 68–69
moodiness:
  female menopause and, 16, 21,
    32–33, 108, 145, 146, 154, 155,
    158, 181
  male menopause and, 48, 107,
    138
Moore, Clement, 206
Moore, Thomas, 191, 192
More, 22
Muir, Charles and Caroline, 189
muscle mass, 54, 76, 95, 107, 202
  male menopause and, 16, 52
music, 38, 172

Nahon, Dr. Danielle, 51–52
National Cancer Institute, 213
National Institute of Aging, 89, 211,
    213
National Institutes of Health, 37, 39,
    211, 213
negativity, 207
Nicholson, Jack, 58
night sweats, 145, 146, 147, 149
Notebook, The (Sparks), 171
Nurses' Health Study, 200
nuts, 200

obesity, 39, 54, 210
omega-3 fatty acids, 197, 199, 200
omega-6 fatty acids, 199

orchitis, 54
organizations, participating in, 63
osteoporosis, 33–35, 42, 202
  bone density tests, 33–34
  female, 21
  prevention and treatment of, 34–35,
    94, 113, 202
  risk factors for, 33
ovarian cancer, 77, 215
ovaries, 153
  surgical removal of, 27–28
oxandrolone, 97
oxytocin, 165–67, 168

painful intercourse, 67, 74, 81, 109,
  110, 155
patience, 150
Paxil, 89
PEA, 167–68
perceptions about changes in ones
  spouse, 13
perimenopause, 12, 46, 77, 108,
  143–53
  determining if your partner is
    entering, 147–49
  finding a physician knowledgeable
    about, 149–50
  helping your partner get through,
    148–53
pets, 38
phenylethylamine, 167–68
pheromones, 166
physical attractiveness, *see* body image
physical examinations, 111
  to determine perimenopause, 147
  males and, 47, 51–52, 86, 90, 107,
    141
Picasso, Pablo, 16
pineal gland, 216
pituitary gland, 28, 94
PMS (premenstrual syndrome), 146
polycystic ovary syndrome, 24

portion control, 40, 198
pravachol, 38
pregnenolone, 215–16
Premarin, 22
preoptic-anterior hypothalamic region,
  28
processed foods, 197
progesterone, 146, 215
prostate and prostate cancer, 47,
  52–53, 58, 90, 94, 95–96, 107,
  201, 215
Prozac, 77, 89
PSA levels, testing, 53, 90, 95–96, 98,
  107
puberty, 100

questionnaires:
  determining your relationship IQ
    (intimacy quotient), 117–19
  how do I know if I'm experiencing
    male menopause, 49–50
  identifying double-menopause
    danger zones, 9–11
  longevity quotient (LQ), 195–96
  midlife sexuality quiz, 70–73
Quinn, Anthony, 58

raloxifene, 39
Randall, Tony, 58
Replens, 75, 150
reproductive endocrinology, 3, 23–24
resentment, getting rid of, 123–24
respect, 185
restaurants, eating at, 40, 198–99
retirement, 102–104, 120, 163
  friendships after, 63
  as trigger of male menopause, 56,
    61–62
retreats, 153
rituals, creating new, 172
Robertson, Anna Mary (Grandma
  Moses), 205–206

Robertson, Dr. Rose, 35–36
romance, midlife, 163–74
    chemistry of, 164, 165–68
    facing reality, 173–74
    igniting our midlife love hormones,
        164–67
    twenty fun ways to activate your
        romance hormones and keep your
        lover, 169–73
romance novels, sharing, 170–71
Rudman, Dr. Daniel, 208

Sarrel, Dr. Phil, 68
saturated fats, 39, 197
scalp massage, 172
scent, power of, 170
Scent of a Woman, The, 170
scorn, 179–80
second honeymoon, 173, 187–89
sedentary lifestyle, osteoporosis and,
    33
selective estrogen receptor modulators
    (SERMs), 39
self-assessment, 186
sensitivity to each other's needs and,
    122–23
separation, 56
serotonin, 173
sexuality, midlife:
    affairs, *see* affairs
    female perspective, *see* midlife
        sexuality, female perspective of
    lack of sexual relations, 12, 73
    longevity and, 205
    male perspective of, *see* midlife
        sexuality, male perspective of
    Tantra sex, 189–90
sexually transmitted diseases,
    183
Shakespeare, William, 113
SHBG (sex hormone-binding
    globulin), 52, 92, 93

Sherwin, Barbara, 32
sildenafil citrate, *see* Viagra
simvastin, 38
skin care, 113
sleep apnea, 96
sleeping habits, 152
sleeping problems:
    depression and, 139
    female menopause and, 16, 22,
        26, 32–33, 108, 145, 146,
        154–55
    hot flashes and, *see* hot flashes
    male menopause and, 2, 48,
        107
    melatonin and, 216
smoking, 152
sodium, 197
sodium fluoride, 34
*Soul Mates: Honoring the Mysteries of
    Love and Relationship* (Moore),
    191
soy, 31, 38–39, 147, 152, 200–201
Sparks, Nicolas, 171
statins, 38
staying connected, 207
steroids, 33, 209, 215
    DHEA, 212–15
stoicism, 31
strength training, 33, 113, 202–203
stress, 54, 149, 152, 202, 207–208,
    214
    methods for lowering, 38
stretching, 204
stroke, 38, 41, 42, 97, 199, 202
    estrogen and, 32
    female, 21, 35
suicide, 139
support groups, male menopause, 3
surgical menopause, 27–28, 32, 75
SWAN (Study of Women's Health
    Across the Nation), 30
Swank, Constance, 68–69

Taber, Andrew, 166
t'ai chi, 34–35, 38, 204
taking each other for granted, avoiding, 185
Tantra, 189–90
testicular cancer, 215
testosterone, 167–68, 215
    depression and, 139
    factors causing decline in males, 54
    female menopause and, 75, 108
    male menopause and, 15–16, 47, 54, 91–98
    overdose, 76, 92, 96
    supplementation for men, 94–98
    supplementation for women, 75–77, 108
    testing levels of, 52, 92–94
thyroid disorders, 94, 211
thyroid medications, 33
Tiegs, Cheryl, 22
time apart and time together, balancing, 106, 124–25, 159, 174
tolerance, lowered threshold of: male menopause and, 16
touch, importance of, 165–67, 169–70
tranquilizers, 22
travel, 174
Treatment of the Post-Menopausal Woman (Lobo), 144
triglycerides, 38, 199
trust, 186
    loss of, 182–84

UCLA School of Medicine, Gerontology Research Laboratory, 197
ulcers, 208
University of California, San Diego Department of Reproductive Medicine, 214

University of California at San Diego, 24
    Clinical Research Unit, 24–25
uterine cancer, 215

Vagifem, 155
vaginal atrophy, 81, 111
vaginal creams, 75, 150
vaginal dryness, 16, 68, 74, 81, 108, 145, 146, 147, 149, 150, 155
    lubrication methods, 74–75, 108, 109, 150, 155
vaginismus, 81
vaginitis, atrophic, 74, 108–109
Valium, 78
vasomotor events, 29
vegetables, 39, 197, 199
vegetarians, 200
vertebral fractures, 34
Viagra, 4, 90
viropause, *see* male menopause
vitamin D, 34
vitamin E, 147, 152
vitamins, 112
VO_2 capacity, 203

Walford, Dr. Roy, 197, 198
Waller, Robert James, 170
Washington University School of Medicine, 203
water, 197
weight, 39, 90, 178, 202, 203
    ideal body, 198
    obesity, *see* obesity
weight-bearing exercises, 33, 113, 202–203
Whitehead, Dr. Malcolm, 68
withdrawal, 180–82
woman's guide to surviving her man's midlife change, 127–42

woman's guide to surviving her man's midlife change (*cont.*)
  author's experience with, 127–31
  being tuned in to his changes, 139
  changes to watch for, 140–41
  depression in males and, 137–39
  renewing your friendship, 141–42
  setting an example for spouse by taking care of yourself, 132, 141
  surviving midlife affair, 136–37
Wyeth Pharmaceuticals, 22

Xanax, 78

yam, Mexican wild, 215
Yen, Dr. Samuel, 214
yoga, 38, 152, 204
Zoloft, 78, 89